*Transforming Stewardship*

TRANSFORMATIONS
THE EPISCOPAL CHURCH IN THE 21ST CENTURY

# Transforming Stewardship

C. K. ROBERTSON

Church Publishing
NEW YORK

Unless otherwise indicated, all passages from the scriptures are from
the *New Revised Standard Version* of the Bible. © 1989 by the
Division of Christian Education of the National Council of Churches
of Christ in the U.S.A. Used by permission. All rights reserved.

Library of Congress Cataloging-in-Publication Data
Robertson, C. K. (Charles Kevin), 1964–
Transforming stewardship / C.K. Robertson.
    p. cm. — (Transformations series)
ISBN 978-0-89869-607-3 (pbk.)
1. Episcopal Church—Finance. 2. Stewardship, Christian—Episcopal
Church. I. Title. II. Series.
BX5961.R63 2009
248'.6—dc22
                                            2008045251

Cover design by Stefan Killen Design.
Study guide and interior design by Vicki K. Black.

*Printed in the United States of America.*

Church Publishing, Incorporated
445 Fifth Avenue
New York, New York 10016
www.churchpublishing.com

        5    4    3    2    1

# Contents

a note from the publisher

This series emerged as a partnership between the Office of Mission of the Episcopal Church and Church Publishing, as a contribution to the mission of the church in a new century. We would like to thank James Lemler, series editor, for bringing the initial idea to us and for facilitating the series. We also want to express our gratitude to the Office of Mission for two partnership grants: the first brought all the series authors together for two creative days of brainstorming and fellowship; and the second is helping to further publicize the books of the series to the clergy and lay people of the Episcopal Church.

# Series Preface

"Be ye transformed" (KJV). "Be transformed by the renewing of your minds" (NRSV). "Fix your attention on God. You'll be changed from the inside out" (*The Message*). Thus St. Paul exhorted the earliest Christian community in his writing to the Romans two millennia ago. This exhortation was important for the early church and it is urgent for the Episcopal Church to heed as it enters the twenty-first century. Be transformed. Be changed from the inside out.

Perhaps no term fits the work and circumstances of the church in the twenty-first century better than "transformation." We are increasingly aware of the need for change as we become ever more mission-focused in the life of the church, both internationally and domestically. But society as a whole is rapidly moving in new directions, and mission cannot be embraced in an unexamined way, relying on old cultural and ecclesiastical stereotypes and assumptions.

This new series, *Transformations: The Episcopal Church in the 21st Century*, addresses these issues in realistic and hopeful ways. Each book focuses on one area within the Episcopal Church that is urgently in need of transformation in order for the church to be effective in the twenty-first century: vocation, evangelism, preaching, congregational life, getting to know the Bible, leadership, Christian formation, worship, and stewardship. Each volume explains why a changed vision is essential, gives robust theological and biblical foundations, offers guidelines to best practices and positive trends, describes the necessary tools for change, and imagines how transformation will look.

For most Episcopalians stewardship is synonymous with pledge drives, budgets, and capital campaigns, but the Bible is clear that God wants more than our tithes and offerings. Looking to its scriptural roots in 1 Chronicles, Luke–Acts, and the letters of Paul, as well as St. Francis's "third way," Robertson offers a vision of holistic stewardship that cannot be separated from evangelism, outreach, Scripture study, and ministry to the newcomer. It involves not strong-arm tactics, but a willingness to embrace new models of generosity and spiritual practices that can transform the church's outmoded attitudes toward stewardship and wealth.

Like Christians in the early church, today we live in a secular culture that can be apathetic and even hostile to Christianity. Living in a setting where people are not familiar with the message or narrative of Christian believing requires new responses and new kinds of mission for the Body of Christ. We believe this is a hopeful time for spiritual seekers and inquirers in the church. The gospel itself is fresh for this century. God's love is vibrant and real; God's mission can transform people's hopes and lives. Will we participate in the transformation? Will we be bearers and agents of transformation for others? Will we ourselves be transformed? This is the call and these are the urgent questions for the Episcopal Church in the twenty-first century.

But first, seek to be transformed. Fix your attention on God. You'll be changed from the inside out.

JAMES B. LEMLER, *series editor*

# Acknowledgments

Although I have authored or edited several books for other publishers, I have long wanted to work with Church Publishing and am deeply grateful for this opportunity to do so. I especially thank the Reverend Doctor James Lemler, editor of the *Transformations* series, for inviting me to join his impressive team of contributors. And I am so very appreciative of the guidance and camaraderie of my editor, Cynthia Shattuck. What a pleasure it is to work with her! I am also very grateful for the excellent work of copyediting and design done by Deacon Vicki Black.

Whatever I have learned about stewardship has come from a few remarkable individuals: Thomas Gossen, Terry Parsons, Glenn Holliman, Charles Gravenstine. They are indeed gifts of God to the church.

Throughout my vocational life, it has never been easy to write books or articles while still working my "day job." At no time has this been more true than now, in my work as Canon to the Presiding Bishop and Primate of the Episcopal Church. I offer thanks, therefore, for the encouragement given me in this endeavor by the Most Reverend Katharine Jefferts Schori. I am thankful for the privilege of working alongside the dedicated colleagues of the

Episcopal Church Center, especially my colleagues in the Presiding Bishop's Office: Ednice Baerga, Miguel Escobar, Sharon Jones, Su Hadden, Neva Rae Fox, and Linda Watt.

This book owes so much to my former parishioners at St. Stephen's Episcopal Church in Milledgeville, Georgia, as well as to the Diocese of Arizona and its bishop, the Right Reverend Kirk S. Smith. Indeed, I remain grateful for all my dear friends who continue to walk with me in this shared journey, especially Gary and Laurie Reichard, Kevin Jamison, Mike Maichak, Michael Rusk, and Mike Rhodes.

I am so deeply thankful for the support and love I continually receive from my wife Debbie and our children, David, Jonathan, and Abigail. And to my Dad, who has always been there for me, I dedicate this book.

# chapter one

# The Current Landscape

*Everyone then who hears these words of mine and acts on them will be like a wise man who built his house on rock. The rain fell, the floods came, and the winds blew and beat on that house, but it did not fall, because it had been founded on rock. And everyone who hears these words of mine and does not act on them will be like a foolish man who built his house on sand. The rain fell, and the floods came, and the winds blew and beat against that house, and it fell—and great was its fall!* (Matthew 7:24–27)

At first glance, the Church of the Foolish and the Church of the Wise appear very similar. Both are proud of their rich heritage and nervous about their uncertain future. A visitor might equally exclaim of either, "What a magnificent sanctuary!" while also adding, "Where are all the people?" It is clear, too, that each of these churches boasts a faithful core of members committed to the care of their spiritual home, their treasure. Yet, in both cases the treasure is costly. As *New York Review of Books* contributor Bill McKibbon notes,

"As GM and Ford bear the weight of old union contracts, the mainline churches bow under the weight of big brick edifices built in an earlier day" (January 17, 2008).

Indeed, the expense of maintaining magnificent *old* buildings has increased considerably through the years even as membership—and the income associated with membership—has declined considerably. In the early 1990s, researcher George Barna noted in *The Frog in the Kettle,* "As the elderly pass away, they are being replaced in the church by generations who have less loyalty to religion, to denominations, to the local churches with which they affiliate and to the very notion of being a formal member of a church."[1] This trend has only increased in the early years of the twenty-first century, as Barna notes in his more recent *Revolution.* Yes, the Church of the Foolish and the Church of the Wise indeed face many similar challenges. Both begin at the same point of origin. It is what they choose to do from there that sets them apart!

The Church of the Foolish does what it has always done: it begs for more money from people who perhaps never truly understood why they gave to begin with, other than for the sake of loyalty. After all, if you belong to a club, you pay the dues. The Church of the Foolish hosts its annual stewardship dinner, because that is what it has always done. In recent years, the church leaders have begun to use prepackaged programs like "The Dogsled Direct." Making the parish hall look and feel like the Arctic (which is not difficult, given the higher heating bills!), a good meal is served, tales are recounted, and a couple of vestry members tell how much this church means to them. And, of course, the treasurer stands up and shows a chart that illustrates how expenses have risen 20 percent, and both salary and insurance rates for a full-time clergyperson have skyrocketed, and things look as dire as they could ever imagine. And then the stewardship chair passes the Dogsled bags out to the people. All this to make the request for money a bit more palatable.

The Church of the Wise faces similar difficulties, but its leaders realize that a new program is not the answer to the larger, long-term problems they face. They refuse to settle for "coyote thinking." I am referring here to the familiar cartoon, in which the wily coyote is always thinking of new ways to snare the seemingly naïve, but ultimately triumphant roadrunner. Hardly unintelligent, the coyote is, in fact, quite innovative and resourceful. He continually comes up with creative stratagems and always utilizes the latest gadgetry (thanks to the endless supplies and instant shipping provided by the Acme Warehouse). The problem with "coyote thinking" is not a lack of ideas, but the inability to review and change one's foundational principles. What amazing things might happen if the coyote decided to become a vegetarian, or even place a take-out order with the local café! All the energy that the coyote expends in his single-minded goal of catching the roadrunner could then be directed toward more creative pursuits, accomplishing great things that remain unimaginable—and thus unattainable—as long as he remains stuck in his familiar paradigm of "catch the roadrunner."

> We do not need a new set of programs. We need churches with a new consciousness of themselves and their task. —Loren Mead

Unlike their Foolish Church neighbors down the street, the leaders of the Church of the Wise have made a conscious decision not to be coyotes in their thinking. Instead, in the language of futurist Joel Barker, they act as *paradigm pioneers,* visionaries who are unafraid to change direction, chart a new course, and ask hard questions. Instead of simply repeating the old refrain, "We wish our church would grow," these wise pioneers go further and ask: "We say we want to grow, but what do we mean by *growth*? If we are talking about adding new members, who is it that we want to attract? We say we want families with young children, but do we know what kind of changes that might mean for us? And *why* do we want to grow? Do we simply want to increase our financial giving base? Are we trying to recapture a past from our nostalgic remembrances? Do we see our congregation as an aging group whose membership needs to be replenished? Or do we find ourselves driven by a gospel imperative to reach out to the unbelieving and the unchurched?" And then there is the issue of *how*: "What will it really take to grow? What changes will we need to implement right now, and what changes will occur as a result of subsequent growth?" The leaders of the Church of the Wise are willing to ask these tough questions.

More than this, they are willing to take a good long look both in the mirror and also outside their walls. In his book *Transforming Congregations for the Future,* Loren Mead of the Alban Institute asserts that we make "idols out of our structures" while failing to ask why the church has "slipped off the radar screens" of so many people in our society. His strong challenge is to acknowledge that we cannot respond to the issues we face as God's ambassadors by doing what we have always done.[2] It is interesting that business leaders have long understood that to which we in the church seem to be oblivious, that past success is the greatest obstacle to future success. This is the exact opposite of what we usually believe: if it worked then, it will work now. But this is simply another form of coyote thinking. Why should we expect past ways and means to work today when we ourselves have changed, individually and corporately? As long as we are focused solely on the protection of what we have or the return to the successes of whatever golden age we recall, we will miss the opportunities of mission and ministry before us. As a wise senior warden once told me, "If there was a golden age, I must have blinked and missed it!" We can celebrate our heritage, learn from our heritage, but we must never get stuck in it.

---

## generation gap

One size does not fit all when it comes to shoes. How much more is this true of people! *The Book of Common Prayer* speaks of "all sorts and conditions" of people, and yet many churches ignore the importance of differences, especially generational differences. A pledge program or capital campaign that works for someone in their sixties will not likely work for someone in their forties, much less someone in their twenties. Researchers separate people into various generational groupings to designate their characteristics and differences. While these groups clearly represent some generalizations that do not accurately describe all those within the respective categories, there are some consistent patterns in the groups which are worth noting:

> ⁺ *Elders:* (also known as Builders and the G.I. Generation). Characterized by Tom Brokaw as "the greatest generation," these are the people who came of age during the Great Depression and the World War II and Korean War years. They are marked by respect for authority, brand loyalty, commitment to save (money), obligation to family (including extended family), traditional values and roles, desire for higher education for their children, and a tendency to stay in one locale ("the family home").

> ⁺ *Baby Boomers:* Born during the postwar baby boom between 1945 and 1963, these are often known as the "Children of the Sixties." Their defining memories are not World War II but the Vietnam conflict,

not FDR but JFK, not Big Band but rock and roll. The most educated generation in American history to that point, these are the progeny of parents who still lived largely traditional roles and spoke of giving their children "the things they did not have." Boomers are marked by their questioning of authority, a hunger for a deep and meaningful spirituality, and the importance of personal relevance.

♦ *Generation X:* The so-called Gen Xer was born during the Age of Aquarius and then came of age during Reaganomics and the rise of neo-conservativism. Witnessing the results of their older siblings' excesses and the domestication of that previous generation's idealism, these baby Gen Xers are strong realists, recognizing the importance of personal control over finances, health care, and retirement. They have more income, yet far less time, and they often complain of stress and burnout. Small groups and a few intimate friends are crucial, while group memberships with demands on time and energy are avoided.

♦ *Millennials:* Also known as Generation Y or Mosaics, this is the most recent group to arrive, and the first generation in a very long time to have a predicted future look more bleak than that of their parents, though technologically, they are the most savvy.

Researchers have become much more insistent that we take seriously the considerable differences between generations, especially when focusing on matters involving group membership, time commitments, and financial giving. Note the following statistics from the Barna research group (www.barna.org):

♦ Millennials are much less likely than any other generation to volunteer time to their church: 12

percent of Millennials report volunteering in the past week, while conversely, 23 percent of Gen Xers, 29 percent of Boomers, and 34 percent of Elders have volunteered in the past week.

✦ Small-group participation appears to be positively correlated with age, with 26 percent of Elders, 24 percent of Boomers, 19 percent of Gen Xers, and 20 percent of Millennials reporting that they participated in a small group in the past week.

✦ Compared to 60 percent of Builders who have a private prayer/devotional time during the week, 54 percent of Boomers, 39 percent of Gen Xers, and 35 percent of Millennials do the same.

✦ 33 percent Millennials, 43 percent of Gen Xers, 49 percent of Boomers, and 53 percent of Elders attend church on a given Sunday.

✦ In a typical week, 32 percent of Millennials, 42 percent of Gen Xers, 47 percent of Boomers, and 58 percent of Elders read the Bible.

✦ In a given week, 65 percent of Millennials, 82 percent of Gen Xers, 90 percent of Boomers, and 88 percent of Elders (Builders and Seniors) report praying to God.

✦ Boomers emerge as more likely (53 percent) and Millennials as less likely (33 percent) than any other generation to be report being "born again" (with 38 percent of Gen Xers and 48 percent of Elders).

✦ Millennials are the least likely age group to indicate that faith is a very important part of their life: only 51 percent of Millennials say their faith is very important in their life, compared with 62 percent of

Gen Xers, 73 percent of Boomers, and 79 percent of Elders.

• Gen Xers are more likely than the other generations to be searching for meaning in life: 44 percent of Gen Xers compared to 32 percent of all others.

• Gen Xers are the generation most likely to feel "too busy": 53 percent of Gen Xers maintain that they are too busy, compared to 49 percent of Boomers, and less than 32 percent of Elders.

• Financial comfort appears to come with age: 38 percent of Gen Xers say they are personally struggling with finances, compared to the 32 percent of Boomers, and less than 23 percent of Elders.

• Gen Xers are almost twice as likely as Elders to indicate that they are "stressed out" (41 percent to less than 27 percent). Likewise, 32 percent of Boomers said that "stressed out" is an accurate description of them.

What is perhaps most interesting about these statistics is how little attention is paid to them by most mainline churches. As a result, congregations continue to use a one-size-fits-all approach to much of what they do, including stewardship. A letter goes out to everyone asking for an increase in their pledges—a single letter saying the same thing. A person gets in the pulpit and tells a story about why pledging is so important to them—one story being told to everyone at once. Yet, as suggested above, the methods and the words that an Elder will appreciate are not likely going to work in the same way with a Boomer or Gen Xer. A more holistic approach to stewardship and education is not only wise, but absolutely necessary. If this is important in terms of the members we already have, it is even more imperative when we begin to look at the people who have not yet come in our doors.

In the years immediately preceding the new century, Lyle Schaller, author of *The Seven-Day-a-Week Church,* looks ahead to speak of the importance of churches focusing on the needs and desires of the unchurched population. There is a desperate need, Schaller goes on to say, for "entrepreneurial, visionary, skilled, energetic, enthusiastic, and persistent" church leaders. Indeed, for far too long mainline churches have appeared to be sleeping giants, displaying little energy for mission imperatives and evangelism. Wise leaders, pioneering leaders, must understand the nature of the people who are *not* attending their services. Lee Strobel, in his book *Inside the Mind of Unchurched Harry and Mary,* paints a picture of the unchurched individual:

- More commonly male than female.

- Either single or married to a person of another religious background.

- More likely to live in a western state.

- Slightly younger median age than the average American.

- Slightly higher median income than the average American.

- More education than the norm.

- Almost always some church experience in their background.[3]

The issue is not necessarily that these unchurched individuals are *against* church. It simply is not relevant in their lives at all. While living in Britain in the 1990s, I discovered a post-religious culture in which at least two generations had no experience within a worship facility apart from baptisms (or "christenings," as they are called there), weddings, and, of course, funerals. The same parish church that is filled to capacity on a Saturday for the funeral of a local villager would be almost completely empty the next day for the weekly service. After a delightful chat on a bus with a man who lived in my village, my closing words, "I look forward to seeing you again soon," were met with a vehement, "Oh, I hope not!" Seeing my surprise, he immediately explained, "If I see you again, it means that someone must have died!" Churches still host many weddings, but more and more "civil unions" are being held in gardens, halls, or homes, and an increasing amount of cohabitating couples see little need for formalizing their relationships at all. Even with baptisms/christenings, churches have begun to see a downturn, as a growing number of people are promoting "naming ceremonies" held in pubs or restaurants, celebrating a new birth without making any specific religious promises or commitments. All this is to say that although there are still active, vital congregations in Britain, their numbers have declined dramatically.

The situation in the United States may appear to be a far cry from what I have just described, especially since the number of churchgoers here is so much larger than in Britain or Europe. But as the statistics above suggest, younger generations in this country are seeing less of a need to belong to a congregation. For more and more people, the question in regards to attending a church is not "Why not?" but "Why?" Even the independent megachurch movement, whose dramatic rise in the past few decades has coincided with the downward plunge of mainline Christianity, is now showing signs of decline.

The Reverend Peter Gomes, renowned preacher and pastor of Memorial Church at Harvard University, argues that twenty-first-century seekers are craving something more: an authentic spiritual experience, life-giving relationships, and a chance to make a difference in the world. In this context, a congregation has to provide something far more meaningful than entertainment. In *The Good Book* as well as his more recent *The Scandalous Gospel of Jesus,* Gomes pushes for a meatier and more realistic faith that is unafraid of the struggles that twenty-first-century people face every day. Gomes calls for church members not only to take a good look at the world outside their walls, but also at the radical message of Jesus and its implications for today. To be effective in mission means appreciating the intersection of Main Street and Church Street, knowing our potential constituency and their needs while also reclaiming our historically rooted, reasonable faith.

This kind of thinking is echoed by Church of England seminary principal Steven Croft, who speaks of "the creation of primary communities in a desert of isolated lives" as the primary task of the local church. Recognizing the dire situation inherent in modern western society—a "white-water society" where change is constant and often overwhelming—Croft calls for the need to "attend to our own inheritance" even as we learn "the lessons of the world around us."[4] A strong grasp of scripture and tradition must balance a reasonable acquaintance with corporate management and leadership development. It has been said that, for many years, denominations and their seminaries were preoccupied with a therapeutic model of ministry, caring for the members already in the church. Returning to Schaller's point from earlier, it is not therapists for insiders that are needed now as much as entrepreneurs seeking to reach outsiders, again "paradigm pioneers" who will help their insiders think outside the box in terms of evangelism and outreach. Croft would add a word of caution: even an entrepreneurial model is inadequate if it is not grounded in and informed by a scripturally and theologically sound foundation. An invisible but real ceiling of congregational growth will block all coyote efforts to recruit and retain newcomers. Just as we do not need more amateur counselors with collars, we also do not need salespersons for Jesus. What we do need is to reorient ourselves to be churches for our communities.

<hr/>

## making a difference

What has just been said does not presuppose that our goal and our context must be the large church only. Far from it! Back in 1982, in their book *Against All Odds: Ten Stories of Vitality in Small Churches,* Charles R. Wilson and Lynne Davenport predicted much of what Peter Gomes and others are now saying. Their experience and focus, however, was the small church setting. Refusing to buy into the "bigger is better" mentality that has pervaded so much of Christianity in recent decades, they listed the characteristics of a vital *small* congregation:

* It is first of all a community—a family—gathered around the Lord's Table.

* There is a healthy relationship of mutual respect with the diocese.

* It has a sense of "who we are and what we are here for"—identity and purpose, together with the administrative skill to organize and implement.

* Outreach is considered an essential element in Christian witness and people are personally involved.

* There is faith and determination in local leaders who can keep things going sometimes in spite of unbelievable odds.

* It benefits from quality in the leadership of the professionally trained career people who move in and

out of its life in various ways—empowering, supporting, helping but not taking over the local ministries.

✦ And finally, it displays the ability to risk, adapt, and change.[5]

Again, note that this list concerns *small* congregations. Vitality, health, and life are not exclusively tied to large churches. Whether the church is large or small, what is needed, quite simply, is intentionality.

This is why vital churches not only have a clear sense of identity but also a clear sense of the importance of making a difference in their community and getting personally involved in the effort. We have to move away from the danger that Dan Dick points to in *Revolutionizing Christian Stewardship for the 21st Century: Lessons from Copernicus,* the danger of putting our energy and resources into the preservation of the status quo. Instead, we need to focus on mission and new possibilities. Would the surrounding community even take notice if our church suddenly closed down? What impact are we making? These questions are being repeated by Melvin Amerson in his look at *Stewardship in African-American Churches,* where he explores new strategies while simultaneously honoring still-relevant traditions. Wilson and Davenport's earlier commendation continues to ring true: "For the neighborhood, the town, or village, the presence of the vital congregation is indeed important." Indeed, from our Anglican heritage, perhaps we can appropriate anew the concept of "the parish church" and become an integral part of our communities, albeit in fresh ways, thereby affirming that evangelism and outreach truly are interconnected. As Michael Hurley-Pitts has argued in his book *The Passionate Steward,* it is time for us to become more critical of our often largely secular practices of fundraising and embrace our call as Christian stewards.

Finally, we have come to the "S" word, the word that most mainline Christians avoid, but also the very word that probably made you pick up this book. So what does stewardship have to do with all the things I have just mentioned? We might as well ask what stewardship has to do with our mission and ministry together as Christians! There is a story about a group of Viking warriors who were ordered by their king to join him when he converted to the Christian faith through the waters of baptism. As they waded out into the nearby river to be baptized, they all went under the water while holding one of their arms high above their heads. If they had been asked why they were doing this, the warriors would have answered that they did not want the arm and hand that bore the sword to go under the water, for they had been taught that whatever goes under the water belongs to God. And these warriors were willing to let the rest of their bodies—and thus their lives—belong to God, but their sword-arms would be held back.

Jesus had it right when he spoke many times about people's money, their treasure: "For where your treasure is, there your heart will be also" (Matthew 6:21). Our wallet and checkbook are precious to us, whether we have little or much. And we protect and worry about what we have, whether it is little or much. Njongonkulu Ndungane, Archbishop of Cape Town, South Africa, has been quoted in Harold T. Lewis's book *A Church for the Future* as saying, "We live in a world in which money has more powerful rights than human rights, a world governed and dominated by Mammon." Mammon, money, is a very potent deity. The same could be said, by the way, of our calendar, appointment book, or scheduler. Indeed, the two are intimately connected, for as the saying goes,

"Time is money." It is all about what we hold dear, what we protect, what we attempt to control at all costs. Those Vikings may not have cared one way or another about the new religion that their king had embraced with them in tow, but they did know that they were not about to give control over the most important part of their life to this new God. One part of their life was definitely not going under the water!

Control is not a bad thing in and of itself, but it is elusive and illusory. Control is a kind of Holy Grail that we are always seeking but that continues to be beyond our grasp... which means we try harder and fret more. In an earlier work, *Religion and Sexuality: Passionate Debates,* I spoke of the ways in which some people see their faith as an "intentional attempt to bring some form of control to an otherwise fearful and fragile existence." We may say, "Let go and let God," when what we really mean is "Get God and get a good life." God becomes a genie of sorts, a cosmic Santa Claus, who gives us a prosperous life if we only believe enough, pray enough, give enough to our church. We gladly go under the water, but not entirely. We are proud of the 2½ percent we give to the church, but the rest belongs to us, and no one—not even God—will tell us what to do with the rest of our time and our treasure. We choose how much of ourselves to hold back. We maintain control. We are Vikings. We are owners.

But, of course, this is not true. We are not owners; we are stewards. Stewards of creation, stewards of our own bodies, stewards of our time and treasure, stewards of "all that we are and all that we have," stewards of one another. A church can be like any individual, seeking control and unconsciously trying to use God in that effort. Such a church will equate stewardship with the annual pledge drive, always with the goal of meeting or increasing the budget, in order to maintain a little more control. Remember, both the Church of the Wise and the Church of the Foolish face the same struggles, the same "changes and chances of this life," as the Prayer Book says. But the Church of the Foolish falls into the dangerous cycle of using whatever new coyote trick it has to try to hold on to what it has, regain whatever golden age it remembers, and find what it believes to be some kind of control.

The book of Proverbs says that "the fear of the LORD is the beginning of wisdom" (9:10). It is only when we realize that we are not in control, that we cannot use God as our personal genie, that life is indeed bigger than us but God is far bigger still—it is only then that we begin to be wise. For it is then that we begin to trade in our myth of a golden age for a desire to make a difference now, both in the life of our own parish and in our surrounding community. It is then that we trade in our fear of losing what we have tried to maintain for a vision of what can be done. Stewardship does indeed deal with money, but it must be far bigger, far more holistic than that. For money is the symbol, the powerful symbol, of our ongoing need for control. But as we begin to think of life in terms of what we *have* instead of what we *lack,* then we can dare to let go of the things that hold us back and strategize together as faithful stewards instead of fearful owners. Then together we are ready to explore our "sacred bundle."

---

### the sacred bundle

This concept stems from a Native American tribal tradition. For a people on the move, dwelling in a region but not defining themselves by it, the bundle was a powerful way to remind themselves of their common identity. Each object in the bundle—seeds, a feather, an ear of corn, an arrowhead—carried within itself a story. Bringing together the elders and members of the tribe, the shaman would open the bundle and spread out the contents, point to each object in turn, and share its significance. By reencountering their common story through the objects in the bundle, these members reaffirmed their heritage, recognized their purpose, and renewed their vision. They were also reminded that there could only be so many items inside the bundle, for it needed to be carried along with them on their ongoing journey. They had to focus on what was truly essential.

The bundle was sacred because the items it contained and the tales they inspired reflected the essence of the tribe's past, present, and future. New insights meant that items might be replaced over time; in this way, the bundle provided both continuity and the possibility of change and new direction. And the shaman's role as carrier of the bundle meant that he or she at times would call the leaders and people back to the essence of who they were and what they were to focus on in their common life. Elders would thus make leadership decisions based on a clear sense of tribal identity.

I first heard of the sacred bundle in a class of second- and third-year seminarians preparing for ordained ministry. It was presented to us as a tool to help churches explore the essential elements of their identity. Like so many others, we all had bought into a hodgepodge of theories about what a church is and how we are to operate in it; we could talk about paradigm shifts and had studied trends and statistics. But this concept offered us something brand new, a fresh way of understanding the landscape in which we would soon be leaders in the midst of extended family-like systems, of modern-day tribes.

It is important to note, however, that there is nothing magical about the bundle itself. It is less of a model than a motif, a way of talking about critical themes such as identity, vision, and mission. Any principles we can glean from such themes are not intended to be in competition with those we learn from the corporate world or from family systems. The fact remains that we are both similar to and more than a business or a family. So-called tribal imagery might prove helpful inasmuch as it is relational yet not overly exclusive. We are called to be something of an extended family that adopts easily and intentionally. We can tap into imagery from our own scriptural heritage, as the sense of tribal or familial connections is prevalent both in the story of ancient Israel and in the life of the early Christian community.

We will, of course, explore much more closely the scriptural foundation of our work in chapter two. For now, however, it might be helpful to summarize much of what has been said by considering some specific instances of the churches of the "foolish" and the "wise."

---

## a tale of many churches

At first glance, St. Clare's looks like the perfect parish. Barely fifteen years old, this suburban church had been created during the last population explosion in the area, and boasted contemporary worship and small study and sharing groups to reach today's overworked and spiritually undernourished professionals. Their founding pastor had died suddenly, and his successor recently left them to take on responsibilities at a larger church.

If you read their parish profile or their monthly newsletter, the first thing you will note is how active several of the lay members are in the leadership of the parish. A second reading will show you that the same names that appeared in leadership lists fifteen years ago are there now. In terms of worship and liturgy, St. Clare's is a mix of contemporary styles, with a noticeable influence from the renewal movement. Parishioners speak quite naturally about the Spirit and quote from the Bible with ease. In the early years of the parish, a fire consumed part of the newly built structure, a fact that remains a common point of reference for all who belong there. In fact, it is almost impossible to have a conversation of any length with a parishioner without the fire coming up at some point.

The other thing that soon becomes noticeable is that the members' giving patterns do not seem to reflect their apparent affluence or the wealth associated with the geographic area of the church. This is a congregation that seems to be forever unable to meet its annual budget, and the addition of a parish hall five years ago—a project that was done "in faith"—has resulted in considerable debt on top of their ordinary expenses.

When I first met with the parish leaders, they told me they had discovered a stewardship plan that worked. "Tell me about it," I responded. They proceeded to tell me of their "Save the Church" campaign last summer. It was quite simple, actually. They stood before the parish during a Sunday service and told them that things were so bad that they would have to close the church if people didn't do something immediately. Some large gifts came in that very week and they were able to eek out their budget for the remainder of the year. As they finished their story, looking quite pleased, I could not help but wonder if they would follow up this year with "Save the Church, Part II."

◆　◆　◆　◆　◆

All Souls' Church is an altogether familiar parish, with beautiful stone craftsmanship matched by equally impressive stained glass, standing in an urban neighborhood that has changed around it. Once renowned for its superb music program, black-and-white photographs of past glories now line the hallway between the sanctuary and the parish hall. Ask any longtime parishioner about the history of All Souls', and they will speak nostalgically of bazaars and socials and one hundred fifty children in Sunday school. A small group of members gathers regularly to polish the brass, trim and edge the lawn, and rearrange the books in the pews.

During the week, the church property is busy and alive with the sound of children in the day school program. A significant revenue source for the church, the school has an excellent program that has won several prestigious awards, and a long waiting list for new students. However, although it bears the name All Souls' Day School and is listed as an "outreach" of the parish, less than a handful of students attend the church and parents simply nod politely when the clergyperson invites them to a parish event. On Sunday mornings, the cheerful noises of the children give way to the hushed tones and reverent tunes of the few who call All Souls' their spiritual home. It has been several years since they started blocking off the last dozen or so pews in order to force worshippers to fill in the empty spots closer to the front and, even so, there is more than enough room to lay out coats and belongings next to them on the pews.

Stewardship is pretty much the same story year in and year out. Each fall, the lay leaders detail the latest costs of repairing the furnace or the need for a new roof. A representative of the endowment committee tells about the difficult times for investors and receives congratulations from the clergyperson for wise handling of the small amount that the parish received years ago and from which the treasurer takes a little more each year to offset the decreasing plate and pledge amounts. Then a letter goes out to the parishioners, the same letter to every member, asking for a little more this year in their pledge. Another letter goes out to the bishop's office, asking for relief of their diocesan assessment and suggestions of grants for which the parish might apply as a historic church. Denial and desperation go hand in hand at All Souls'. The non-scriptural parable of the little train engine that could is an unspoken theme: will they make it another year? They think they can, they think they can.

◆ ◆ ◆ ◆ ◆

For decades St. Grantham's has enjoyed its reputation as the largest church in the diocese. The other churches all look to it as the "cardinal parish" because of its large staff, it many programs, and its prestige. Its members largely take for granted these same attributes and are clear that they came to this parish precisely because it is "successful" and can meet their spiritual, relational, and vocational needs. A large and respected kindergarten-through-eighth-grade school is on the premises, a school with its own governing board and its own aspirations. The previous rector is something of a legend, having raised money with little effort to build the campus. His method of stewardship was simple: locate wealthy donor prospects and build relationships with them. He was known both within and outside the parish as the priest with the Midas touch. Indeed, he was so successful in his efforts that any general stewardship efforts were largely seen as unnecessary, and overall pledges remained flat.

When a new priest finally came to the parish, he struggled for the first few years in the shadow of his illustrious predecessor. As he spent time looking around him, however, this new pastor saw the needs around him. Though the parish appears at first glance to be in great shape, the fact is that while there are a lot of part-time priests helping with the worship services and teaching forums, the full-time staff is actually far too small to serve a corporate-sized operation, and staff members have been exhibiting signs of burnout. Parishioner participation in the leadership of the parish needs to increase, and the financial base broadened . . . but how? And how can they include the school in whatever plans they develop? As this priest was learning, the situation would involve far more than simply a new pledge campaign. Stewardship at St. Grantham's would have to include vision and leadership and ownership on the part of everyone. Again, the only question was, "How?"

♦    ♦    ♦    ♦    ♦

In these and countless other real-life scenarios, the ongoing challenge is to move from the patterns of the Church of the Foolish to embrace the ways of the Church of the Wise. The solution is simple, but by no means easy, for it usually involves change, and change never comes easily. However, the alternative is unacceptable. As former U.S. Army Chief of Staff General Eric Shinseki has said, "If you don't like change, you're going to like irrelevance a lot less." To be a Church of the Wise means taking seriously the need for change. It means taking into account the issues that we considered in this initial chapter, as well as discerning the types of stewardship resources and tools that are available to be used. It means discovering a theology of stewardship that is sound and strong, and developing an overall strategy that is holistic and realistic. Thus, it is to these things—these crucial steps in the journey to wisdom—that we now turn.

# chapter two

# Tour Guides

*We need to attend to our own inheritance if a new and
healthy understanding of what it means to be ordained is
to emerge. —Steven Croft*

All too often, when we hear about stewardship, it is
only the tithe that is discussed. God, however, is
concerned with much more than ten percent of our
possessions. Indeed, in the words of the Prayer Book, God
cares about "all that I am and all that I have." What then
does this mean? What does it mean to be a steward of all
that we are and all that we have? What does God have to
say about money and wealth and responsibility and relationships? What would a larger, more comprehensive
understanding of stewardship look like, and where do
financial considerations fit in such an understanding?
These are important questions and worthy of study.

The word "steward" is strongly linked to the notion of
a "household." Indeed, the Greek word usually translated
as steward, *oikonomós,* is derived from the word for
"household," *oikía.* For Luke and the other New
Testament writers, an *oikonomós* was the manager of
household affairs. Individuals in this position were

entrusted by the head of the household with management of household affairs and expenditures, as well as the oversight of other workers and even underage children. It is interesting to see how the word *oikonomós* has been translated into English. Although the architects of the King James Version of the Bible chose the term "steward" in the majority of uses, they also resorted to such different terms as "chamberlain" and "governor." The choice of "manager" in many contemporary versions appears to catch some of Luke's meaning, though the Greek word still carries with it greater relational depth. This is evident in Luke 12:42: "Who then is the faithful and prudent manager [steward] whom his master will put in charge of his slaves, to give them their allowance of food at the proper time?" A steward shows care and concern for others.

In this chapter we explore the scriptural and theological foundations of a more holistic approach to stewardship, focusing on wise and faithful stewards—tour guides—such as David, Barnabas, and Francis of Assisi. Here we will thus lay a strong groundwork for the strategic and practical applications that are the focus of the next chapter.

---

## "all things come from you"

> But who am I, and what is my people, that we should be able to make this freewill offering? For all things come from you, and of your own have we given you. (1 Chronicles 29:14)

David's song of praise in 1 Chronicles is well known to Episcopalians—and for good reason. For many years, through various revisions of the Prayer Book, the people's freewill offerings have been brought before the Holy Table with these words: "All things come of thee, O Lord, and of thine own have we given thee." Like the traditional version of the Lord's Prayer, it is the other piece of Elizabethan English that survives and finds it way unbidden into otherwise contemporary worship services, as well as into the corporate memory of congregations. I believe there is something appropriate—something "meet and right"—about the survival of these words from 1 Chronicles, inasmuch as they just might represent the clearest foundational statement of stewardship in the scriptures.

---

All tithes from the land, whether the seed from the ground or the fruit from the tree, are the LORD's; they are holy to the LORD. *(Leviticus 27:30)*

---

This is significant since all too often it is the "biblical tithe" that catches people's attention. This makes sense, inasmuch as dealing with ten percent of our possessions might be far less threatening than wrestling with one hundred percent. Yet for all the attention that the tithe receives in churches, making a strong case for it actually involves something of a scavenger hunt of various verses. The first canonical mention of the tithe is in one of the most ambiguous of biblical passages, a fascinating story in Genesis about the meeting of the progenitor Abraham with the mysterious Melchizedek, priest-king of Salem (14:18–20). After a significant military victory, Abraham encounters Melchizedek, who blesses him. Then Abraham "gave him one tenth of everything." Many pages have been devoted to the question of the problematic pronouns: Who exactly is the "he" who tithes, and who is the "him" to whom the tithe is given? The epistle to the Hebrews argues that the one offering the tithe is Abraham, thereby illustrating that the traditional levitical priesthood of Israel is actually of a lesser quality than the eternal priesthood of Melchizedek (7:4–10). It could be argued that what is important here is not who did the tithing but why it was done, for it clearly involves a spirit of genuine thanksgiving.

There are other passages in the Torah, the Law of Moses, that address the specific logistics of how the tithe was to be offered in the life of ancient Israel. Leviticus 27:30–32 delineates how the tithe of fruits, grains, vegetables, or animals was to be considered as something holy, set apart for the God who watches over them. Numbers 18:24–26 refers to the unique role of the Levites who received "a tithe of the tithe," since they had no land apportioned to them as did the other tribes. Deuteronomy 12 and 14 speak of the context of the offering of the tithe in the midst of a service of praise and rejoicing. For subsequent generations, as mentioned in passages such as 2 Chronicles 31:5–6 and Nehemiah 10:35–39, Israel returned to the tithe as a sign of both appreciation and devotion to God. Malachi calls out to the people, suggesting that in ceasing to tithe they are indeed "robbing God." The solution was to break the curse by bringing tithes in the storehouse or treasury, and God will once again "open the windows of heaven for you and pour down for you an overflowing blessing" (3:8–10).

In the midst of these scattered passages, the voice of the prophet Amos sarcastically points to the hypocrisy of Israel's tithing while simultaneously committing all manner of transgressions (4:4–5). This is a theme that is echoed in the gospels, as Jesus clearly rebukes the "faithful" tithers of his time who simultaneously neglect the greater matters of justice, mercy, and love (Matthew 23:23; Luke 11:42). The second-century martyr Justin makes much of this hypocrisy in his *Dialogue with Trypho,* while another early church father, Irenaeus, points out in his apologetic work *Against Heresies* that Jesus always went much further than any simplistic legalism: "Instead of the law promoting the giving of tithes, [Jesus told us] to share all our possessions with the poor" (13.3).

Indeed, in the gospels, conversion is linked to one's attachment with possessions, as seen in the story of the rich young ruler who approaches Jesus with the question of how to enter heaven (Luke 18:18–25). Jesus is disturbingly clear in his response, "Sell all that you own and distribute the money to the poor, and you will have treasure in heaven; then come, follow me." We are told that the rich man could not follow through on his desire to follow Jesus: "When he heard this, he became sad; for he was very rich." Conversion, for Jesus, is not something to be talked about or internalized—it is a choice that carries with it visible ramifications. It is hard work, further complicated by the addition of wealth: "It is easier for a camel to go through the eye of a needle than for someone who is rich to enter the kingdom of God."

> Will anyone rob God? Yet you are robbing me! But you say, "How are we robbing you?" In your tithes and offerings! You are cursed with a curse, for you are robbing me—the whole nation of you! Bring the full tithe into the storehouse, so that there may be food in my house, and thus put me to the test, says the LORD of hosts; see if I will not open the windows of heaven for you and pour down for you an overflowing blessing.... Then all nations will count you happy, for you will be a land of delight, says the LORD of hosts. *(Malachi 3:8–12)*

Hard work, indeed...yet possible. This is displayed positively in the delightful story of Zacchaeus, the "vertically challenged" chief tax collector who wants desperately to see Jesus (Luke 19:1–10). Luke makes sure that we know that Zacchaeus is not simply an average, run-of-the-mill revenue collector; he states quite clearly that Zacchaeus is "rich." However, unlike the rich young ruler, Zacchaeus breaks through his own limitations, physically and spiritually. He climbs a sycamore tree to catch a glimpse of this celebrity about whom he has heard so much, only to find that Jesus not only notices him, but even invites himself to the tax collector's home. The climatic scene in the man's house is a classic Lukan illustration of conversion. Zacchaeus publicly recognizes the fact that he has wronged many in the past and vows in the presence of all his guests to make fourfold restitution. Formerly clenched fists have become open hands.

Unlike the rich young ruler, who had all the right words but could not let go of the possessions that actually possessed him, Zacchaeus displays a heart that has become rich toward God through visible, intentional action. Similarly, when Jesus sees "rich people putting their gifts into the treasury" at the temple in Jerusalem (Luke 21:1–4)—giving their tithe as they were expected to do— he points to the poor widow whose seemingly small offering of only two coins is the true gift, since she has given "all she had to live on." These and many other passages point to the fact that God, who has not withheld any good thing from us but indeed has "so loved the world that he gave his only Son" (John 3:16), is concerned with all that we are and all that we have, not simply ten percent!

Thus, we return to that key passage about stewardship in the Hebrew scriptures, and the song of David that has become forever ensconced in our own worship. "All things come from you, O God, and of your own have we given you." *All* things. What is the context for these words? Throughout the chronicler's account, David is always depicted as the great king, the exemplar of leadership in Israel against which all subsequent rulers would be judged (and usually found wanting). You won't find the story of his lust for Bathsheba in 1 Chronicles! The emphasis in the Chronicles is not on David's foibles and failings, but on his triumphs and devotion to God. There, the most important act of David is not a particular military or political victory, but rather his declaration that "a house for the Lord" should be built in the newly appointed capital, Jerusalem. It is almost irrelevant that the one who actually builds the temple is David's son (by Bathsheba, no less!). No, to the author of the Chronicles it is David who is the true architect and engineer, and the service of thanksgiving in the twenty-ninth chapter is, in a way, a temple dedication celebration in advance. Both the service and David's life story culminate with his words of praise and blessing: "Yours, O LORD, are the greatness, the power, the glory, the victory, and the majesty" (29:11). It is crucial that the people of Israel know what—or rather who—is behind their successes.

David's final words, "Who am I, and what is my people?" (29:14) are to be viewed, then, not as mere self-deprecation, but as words filled with awe and profound gratefulness in the light of the intimate relationship that the people have with the Divine. With this in mind, the people's offerings are to be viewed not in terms of obligation, but appreciation. The New Testament proclamation that "we love because God first loved us" (1 John 4:19) echoes this. So, too, do all the various gospel passages concerning those who reveal their transformed lives through their joyful giving. What a contrast to our "earning culture," in which the payment of any tax is a begrudgingly fulfilled duty since we do not want to let go of our hard-earned money. The first step in being God's steward, the first conversion moment, is when we, like David and Zacchaeus and the poor widow in the temple, recognize that what we have, whether little or much, truly is a divine gift. Perhaps this is why Jesus, the Son of David, speaks so often in his parables of stewards—those who know that what they have is ultimately not theirs, not earned as much as entrusted.

The fact, then, that it is *David* who declares that "all things come from you, O God" is not insignificant, for here is the ultimate "Type-A" individual in the Hebrew scriptures. From the moment we encounter him, David is hard at work: tending sheep, fighting Goliath, working for the king, leading a band of guerilla fighters, taking on the role of monarch, uniting the people under one govern-ment. This is not a person who sits back and waits for someone to give him something; this is a can-do person who goes after what he wants and usually gets it. How easy it is for us in our busy lives to fall into the trap of believing that everything is up to us, and so we have to clutch whatever we have close to our heart so that we do not lose it. We work, we earn, we own. Again, as I have said already, God is God...so we don't have to be! Moving from a position of ownership to one of steward-ship really is liberating, for like David we can choose to move from a position where we are at the center total responsibility—and the anxiety that accompanies it—to a place where we can still work hard but at the same time let go, turning clenched fists into open hands of praise and giving.

## "all things were held in common"

In the opening chapters of Acts, the twelve apostles and the community that surrounds them display an almost communalistic approach to possessions, in which their money and goods are viewed as gifts of God to be shared for the good of all rather than treasures to be stored up.

> Now the whole group of those who believed were of one heart and soul, and no one claimed private ownership of any possessions, but everything they owned was held in common. *(Acts 4:32)*

More than this, the apostles are seen at the end of Acts 4 as being integrally involved in the reception and distri-bution of those goods. This fits with what we have already seen in stories found in Luke's gospel, where a converted life is visibly represented by a radical new approach to one's treasures. Indeed, although Luke shares with

Matthew many of the same injunctions and stories about the danger of trusting in possessions—material not found in Mark's gospel—Luke places these otherwise disparate sayings into one "sermon" in Luke 12. The result in reading Luke 12 is that it offers a fairly consistent message about the danger of trusting in apparent financial security. As with Matthew, Luke emphasizes the need to be spiritually focused and prepared:

|  | LUKE | MATTHEW |
|---|---|---|
| Words about fear | 12:2–9 | 10:29–36 |
| Blasphemy against the Spirit | 12:10–12 | 12:31–32 |
| Inheritance squabbles | 12:13–15 | |
| Parable of the storehouses | 12:16–21 | |
| Do not worry about your life | 12:22–31 | 6:25–33 |
| Where your treasure is | 12:32–34 | 6:20–21 |
| Parable of prepared slaves | 12:35–38 | 25:1–13 |
| Parable of housebreaking | 12:39–40 | 24:43–44 |
| Peter's question to Jesus | 12:41 | |
| Parable of faithful steward | 12:42–48 | 24:45–51 |

It is intriguing, however, to note the importance of the uniquely Lukan aspects of this section, stories that have no clear parallel in Matthew. The tale of the brothers vying for the family inheritance suggests a lack of care and mutual love that should otherwise have been assumed for family members. The subsequent parable of the rich man who puts his energy and his trust in his own fiscal preparations for the future suggests the foolishness of a life in which God is ignored and riches are idolized. Even where Luke and Matthew share the same material—Jesus' words regarding the birds of the air and lilies of the field—the Lukan version notes that the audience is not the unnumbered multitudes of Matthew's Sermon on the Mount, but rather "his disciples" (Luke 12:22, as contrasted with Luke's earlier mention of "the crowd" in 12:13). As in Matthew's Sermon, Jesus in the Lukan account assures his disciples that their heavenly Father both knows and will supply their needs. Luke, however, adds one more intriguing and crucial note: "Sell your possessions, and give alms" (12:33). In the Old Testament, almsgiving had been a tangible form of compassion, as seen in both the Psalms ("Happy are those who consider the poor," 41:1) and Proverbs ("Those who oppress the poor insult their Maker, but those who are kind to the needy honor God," 14:31). In Acts, Luke offers several examples of Zacchaeus-like people whose converted lives are precisely evident in their almsgiving. Tabitha of Joppa (9:36), Cornelius the God-fearing centurion (10:2), and Paul of Tarsus (24:17) are all described explicitly as almsgivers.

But the early chapters of Acts describe something far beyond almsgiving. The converts on the day of Pentecost immediately begin to display a radical change in life by selling their possessions and bringing the proceeds to the apostles, so that those among them in need may be aided (2:44–46). An almost identical tale is related in Acts 4, suggesting that, for Luke, Pentecost was not simply a one-time event, but rather an ongoing experience among the Jerusalem believers:

> With great power the apostles gave their testimony to the resurrection of the Lord Jesus, and great grace was upon them all. There was not a needy person among them, for as many as owned lands or houses sold them and brought the proceeds of what was sold. They laid it at the apostles' feet, and it was distributed to each as any had need. (4:33–35)

This kind of giving goes beyond general almsgiving, beyond what is usually called "outreach" in today's churches, for the recipients of financial help here are not the unknown poor, but fellow members of the community. Here, it is not Psalm 41 or Proverbs 14 that provides Old Testament precedents, but rather Deuteronomy 15:

> If there is among you anyone in need, a member of your community in any of your towns within the land that the LORD your God is giving you, do not be hard-hearted or tight-fisted toward your needy neighbor. (Deuteronomy 15:7)

In similar words, Leviticus 25:35 states: "If any of your kin fall into difficulty and become dependent on you, you shall support them." In the words of the well-known religious folk song, "And they'll know we are Christians by our love." The most powerful and visible argument for the truths the apostles proclaimed was not the deeds of power that accompanied their message, but rather how Luke described the church community: "There was not a needy person among them" (Acts 4:34). Miracles astound and amaze, but a community that truly takes care of its own is itself a miracle. Justin Martyr proclaims in his *Apology*, "We who once coveted the wealth of others now place in common the goods we possess" (14.2–3).

It should be noted that what Luke and Justin report was not unknown in the ancient world. Over three centuries before the coming of Christ, Aristotle quoted the proverbial saying "Friends' goods are common property," commenting that even as members of a family hold "all things in common," so do members of a close community (*Nicomachean Ethics* 8.9). The Jewish historian Josephus, in his *Jewish War*, provides what is perhaps the most fascinating analogy in his account of another first-century Jewish sect, the Essenes:

> They have a law that new members on admission to the sect shall confiscate their property to the order, with the result that you will nowhere see either abject poverty or inordinate wealth; the individual's possessions join the common stock and all, like members of the same family, enjoy a single patrimony. (2.122)

Josephus's high regard for the Essenes is clear and perhaps overly idealistic. As is evident in the chilling tale about the greedy, dishonest pledgers Ananias and Saphira in Acts 5, Luke is more honest about the not-so-idyllic reality of the Jerusalem church. But it is intriguing that these exemplars of greed and deceit are introduced immediately after the debut of a character who is Luke's model of a real and holistic stewardship, our tour guide *par excellence,* "a Levite, a native of Cyprus, Joseph, to whom the apostles gave the name Barnabas (which means 'son of encouragement')" (Acts 4:36).

Barnabas first appears as a disciple who, having a field that belonged to him, sells it and brings the proceeds from that sale in full, laying them at the feet of the apostles (Acts 4:37). Some points should be noted about this statement. First, the phrase "at the feet" (*para toús pódas*) is a significant one for Luke, who uses it to denote both a sense of devotion or reverence that the giver has for the receiver and the trustworthiness of the receiver. It is a phrase found most often in Luke–Acts; indeed, over 43 percent of all New Testament occurrences of *pódas* or "feet" occur in Luke's two-volume work. The Fourth Gospel also makes use of *pódas,* but usually in the symbolic context of service, such as the anointing of Jesus' feet by Mary of Bethany (John 12:3) and the washing of the disciples' feet by Jesus himself (John 13:5). Luke instead focuses on the reverential theme of individuals at the feet of Jesus: to listen to him teach (the Gerasene demoniac, 8:35, and Mary the sister of Martha, 10:39); to seek help from him (Jairus, 8:41); to offer thanks for healing already received (the Samaritan leper, 17:16). In each case, the imagery of being at the feet of Jesus clearly conveys a sense of deep devotion. This sense of devotion is also found in Acts, most notably in the story of the centurion Cornelius, who prostrates himself at the feet of

Peter (10:25), and in Paul's claim that he had once studied "at the feet of Gamaliel" (22:3).

However, "at the feet" is also used in Acts to denote the entrusting of possessions to another who is deemed trustworthy, as when the witnesses at Stephen's stoning lay their cloaks "at the feet of a young man named Saul" (7:58), trusting him to watch over them. Both trust and respect are clearly conveyed in the twin instances of followers laying their money at the feet of the apostles (4:35, 37). The mention of the apostles' powerful testimony to the resurrection (4:33), far from being a break in thought in the midst of Luke's discussion on the sharing of possessions, actually serves to show how they exercised both spiritual and social leadership in that communal system. Under the apostles' leadership, the gospel message was preached *and* the needs of all in the community were met through the distribution of funds (4:35). Whether the apostles were the direct overseers of the fund or not, Luke makes it clear that it was to the apostles that financial gifts such as Barnabas's were entrusted and distribution made. The Jerusalem leaders were entrusted with the money, which is another way of saying that they were entrusted with the stewardship of the congregation.

Thus, we see that Barnabas was one of an unnumbered group of followers who sold what they owned, gave of the proceeds through a system in some way involving the leadership of the twelve, and thereby displayed a mutual care for one another. When Acts 4:32 declares that the believers were "of one heart and soul," what is actually declared in the Greek is that there was "one heart and soul in the multitude of those who believed." This is more than a common purpose; it is a common life. In the same way that the presentation of the proceeds at the feet of the apostles is symbolic of an internal reality—the great reverence that the Jerusalem Christians felt toward their leaders—even so their outward giving points to their awareness of the interwoven nature of their lives in Christ. In 1 Corinthians 12, Paul uses the image of the human body to describe a profound kind of Christian unity; here Luke depicts the same in narrative form. Indeed, what the Jerusalem believers exhibited in their giving is nothing less than a deep sense of their mutual interdependence.

If, however, this was the end of Barnabas in the book of Acts, it might very well have also been the end of the Christian movement, for despite the remarkable success of the leaders of the Jerusalem church, they themselves unwittingly set limits to their own success. Yes, Luke is clear that wherever these "uneducated and ordinary men" (4:13) spoke, crowds turned into converts. Yes, he is clear that these previously impotent disciples now acted as living conduits of "signs and wonders" (2:43; 5:12). But Luke is also clear that all their preaching, all their power, and all their success *were confined to Jerusalem, their comfort zone.*

From the moment that Jesus promises the apostles the gift of empowerment by the Holy Spirit, they ask if this would be the time when God would restore the kingdom to Israel (Acts 1:6). Even after all they had seen and experienced, their thoughts about Jesus and his mission were still quite limited. Jesus responded by attempting to replace their missionary myopia with a much broader vision: "You will receive power when the Holy Spirit has come upon you; and you will be my witnesses in Jerusalem, in all Judea and Samaria, and to the ends of the earth" (1:8). These words of Jesus were more provocative than prophetic, for although the apostles and their converts were continually blessing God, Luke explicitly states that they did so "in the temple" (Luke 24:53). Similarly, even as they began a new routine of breaking bread in private homes, they still spent time each day in the temple (Acts 2:46). The healing of a lame man occurred at the Beautiful Gate as Peter and John "were going up to the temple at the hour of prayer" (Acts 3:1). Peter addressed the people at Solomon's Portico (3:11; 5:12), and after their release from the authorities, the twelve returned daily to the temple (5:42). Later, during the persecution that followed Stephen's death, all the disciples were scattered throughout Judea and Samaria, taking the message of Jesus with them—all, that is, but the twelve (8:1). Having once been told by Jesus to wait in the city (Luke 24:49), the Lukan twelve do just that! Thus, they appear to have been perfectly open to the first part of Christ's commissioning—"You will receive power when the Holy Spirit has come upon you; and you shall be my witnesses"—but incapable of hearing the second part—"in Jerusalem, in all Judea and Samaria, and to the ends of the earth."

It is not insignificant, then, that Barnabas is described in his debut as being from Cyprus. Unlike the apostles, his primary spoken language was not Aramaic, but Greek. His version of the scriptures was not the Hebrew *Tanakh,* but the Greek Septuagint. His life experience was not limited to the provincial towns dotting the Sea of Galilee, but the far-flung communities of the Mediterranean. Matthias the insider may have been the one chosen by lots to replace Judas as an apostolic witness (Acts 1:26), but it was Barnabas from Cyprus who helped the church family that had adopted him fulfill its commission. It is Barnabas who showed that holistic stewardship means far more than filling out a pledge card!

How did he do this? The answer lies in the subsequent appearances Barnabas makes in Acts. After five chapters offstage, he first reappears following the tale of Saul's conversion in Acts 9. This Saul is the same young man who once stood by at the stoning of Stephen and at whose feet the executioners placed their cloaks. He went on to take an even more direct role in the prosecution and persecution of followers of Jesus. Is it any wonder, then, that even after hearing of Saul's conversion on the Damascus Road, the apostles in Jerusalem still wanted nothing to do with him? He clearly was not the kind of newcomer they were looking for, certainly not someone to trust. The only reason that the twelve were willing to have a face-to-face meeting with Saul at all was that their major contributor, the "son of encouragement," vouched for him. Luke does not offer a reason why Barnabas suddenly appeared, nor why he stood up for Saul. It really does not matter. The fact is there probably would be no "apostle Paul" if Barnabas the encourager, Barnabas the steward of others, had not stood up for him.

Then Barnabas went to Tarsus to look for Saul, and when he had found him, he brought him to Antioch. So it was that for an entire year they met with the church and taught a great many people, and it was in Antioch that the disciples were first called "Christians." *(Acts 11:25–26)*

Barnabas did more than simply welcome the newcomer. He also nurtured the giftedness and leadership potential in Saul. In an interesting plot twist in his narrative, Luke reports that followers of Jesus suddenly found themselves on the run as a result of the death of the protomartyr, Stephen. For a follower of Jesus, Stephen's martyrdom marked a watershed moment, as it suddenly had become very dangerous indeed to belong to this new inclusive movement. It should be noted that the stoning of Stephen came as a direct result of his sermon, the longest in the book of Acts, which concludes with the suggestion that the Jerusalem temple really was irrelevant. This was the very thing the Pharisees feared all along: that the new "Jesus movement" would somehow render as unimportant all the laws that separated devout Jews from the outsiders, the Gentiles among whom they lived. Now, as they departed from Jerusalem, the various believers brought the new faith with them, and that is how it found its way to Antioch. There, it was not only the Jews who were recipients of their evangelistic efforts, but Gentiles also. In an understated verse, Luke says that it was in Antioch that they were first called "Christians" (Acts 11:26).

When the apostles heard of the dramatic success in Antioch, they decided to send a representative, an ambassador, to check on things and provide a connection between the new believers and the Jerusalem leadership. Their choice in a representative was—no surprise here—Barnabas. What is more surprising is that on his way to his new assignment, this bridge-builder took a detour to Tarsus, where he sought out the very person the apostles earlier avoided: Saul. For Barnabas, it was not enough that Saul had met the Jerusalem leaders; now it was time to put him to work. His decision once again illustrates excellent stewardship on Barnabas's part, for he obviously saw in this cocky upstart the kind of leadership gifts that could be well utilized in a new church plant.

The story of Barnabas thus develops along a fascinating line, from making a substantial financial gift and entrusting it to the apostles for the support of the community, to reaching out to the newcomer that no one else wants to include, to nurturing Saul's leadership so that he in turn moves from newcomer to useful worker. Later in Acts, we find Barnabas doing one of the hardest things of all: he takes second place to Paul's leadership, as Luke's phrase "Barnabas and Saul" becomes "Paul and Barnabas." A true steward, Barnabas displays a humility that may not have come naturally, but was necessary if he really wanted to see the new communities built up in the most effective ways. He could choose to cling to the leadership role bestowed on him by the apostles and accepted by the believers in Antioch. Instead, he continues to do what he has done from the start: discern the need, and then do whatever it takes to meet that need—even if it means laying his ego, like his possessions, at the feet of Christ.

Humility and openness are likewise evident when Barnabas and Saul are singled out by their colleagues in Antioch after a time of prayer and fasting. In fact, in Luke's terminology, Barnabas and Saul are *apostoléo*, "sent out," by those praying believers. A few words should be said about apostleship in Luke-Acts. It is a favorite term of Luke's. To be more specific, over half of all the New Testament appearances of "apostle" in its different variations (*apostoloús*—eight out of fifteen, *apostoloí*—ten out of sixteen, *apostolōn*—thirteen out of twenty-two) are in Luke's two-volume work. For Luke, to be an apostle is to be a witness who proclaims by word and deed the good news of God in Christ. In Jerusalem, apostleship was somehow linked with the past, with the glory days of Israel. This is evident in the choice of Matthias, so that the number of apostles could match the number of tribes; likewise, the apostles stayed close to the temple, insiders all. In Antioch, the focus moved to the future, from insiders to outsiders. It is no accident that Antioch, without a focus on temple and tradition and insiders, was the very place where the newly named Christian community comprised both Jews and Gentiles. It is from Antioch that Paul and Barnabas are chosen and sent out as apostles to as-yet-unformed communities of Gentiles and Jews alike. For different reasons, both Barnabas of Cyprus and Saul of Tarsus are outsiders in Jerusalem, but in Antioch they are the perfect choice for apostolic work. Thus, Luke displays a new, more efficient formula for evangelism and church growth. Barnabas the one-time newcomer welcomes and develops Saul the controversial newcomer, and together they are sent out to find and build up a next generation of newcomers. Barnabas the steward is, by definition, Barnabas the encourager, the church-grower, the apostle.

This is healthy, holistic stewardship where we move from a clenched fist, not simply with money but with people and their gifts, to an open hand that reaches out, brings in, and builds up. Luke records that Paul and Barnabas eventually part company over the issue of including John Mark, a follower who earlier let them down. Whatever the negative ramifications of the separation, it is significant that the final image of Barnabas in Acts is, once again, as a cheerleader for the unwanted.

The picture of Barnabas that is drawn by Luke in Acts is that of a person who puts others before himself, who makes intentional choices to trust, encourage, and empower. Financial pledging is not the goal for Barnabas, but a starting point and a means. The goal is always the building up of the community of believers who together can have an impact on the world around them. Barnabas is a generous donor, a recruiter and retainer of newcomers, an empowering encourager of new leadership, a team player, a person committed to the power of prayer, an agent for change, an ambassador to the world around him, an apostle. In short, Barnabas is Luke's model of a holistic steward.

We turn now to another tour guide, one who lived many years after Barnabas but a steward whose life would epitomize the very qualities that Barnabas modeled. A soldier and merchant's son, this next guide became one of the most famous of all Christian heroes, Francis of Assisi.

"blessed be God, from whom all good things come"

Born Giovanni Bernadone in 1181, this son of a wealthy fabric trader in the Italian hills would be far better known by the nickname bestowed by his father in honor of his French-bred mother. He was barely twenty-one when he set off for fame and honor as a knight in the wars. His chivalric dreams were dashed, however, as the would-be knight was captured, imprisoned, and left to rot for several months as a prisoner of war. It was a broken man who emerged from the dungeons and found his way home to parents and friends who could not grasp what he had experienced. Thankfully, his story does not end there. Hearing a passage from Matthew 10 read in church one day, Francis made the fateful decision to renounce his inherited wealth and live a life of simplicity, chastity, and poverty. "Rebuild my church," he heard the voice of God tell him, and the joy with which he responded to this call was contagious, with followers soon finding their way to him.

As you go, proclaim the good news, "The kingdom of heaven has come near." Cure the sick, raise the dead, cleanse the lepers, cast out demons. You received without payment; give without payment. Take no gold, or silver, or copper in your belts, no bag for your journey, or two tunics, or sandals, or a staff; for laborers deserve their food. *(Matthew 10:7–10)*

At the heart of Francis's message was the notion that all good things come from a good and loving God, and thus all are linked together in a profound network of relationships. Sun and moon, wind and rain, all were seen by Francis as brothers and sisters, fellow siblings of one, loving Creator. All of life became an adventure to be treasured, a series of divinely anointed gifts to be experienced and shared. His first Rule, the *Regula Primitiva,* had twenty-four chapters and represented a balance between his belief that the community gathering around him had to operate firmly within the context of the Catholic Church and his passion for living the gospel life through poverty, preaching, and purity of life. Though he stated unequivocally in the final paragraph that nothing was to be added to this Rule and there would be no other Rule for his followers, only a few years later he indeed drafted a new Rule, one that—unlike the first—would be officially sealed and sanctioned through a papal bull, thereby giving it the name *Regula Bullata.* This Rule, though more acceptable to the papal legalists thanks to the dispensing of much of the sermon-like material and a formulizing of the more passionate language of the first Rule, still conveyed Francis's focus on an apostolic lifestyle through poverty for his followers.

He himself referred to his movement at times as *religio,* or a religious movement like the Benedictines or Augustinians, though his band were never tied to one spot, as most monks were. Those earliest Franciscans were on the move, taking the gospel message with them wherever they went. At the same time, they were a "fraternity," the other term used by Francis to describe his "band of brothers." With the coming of Clare and her order of "Poor Clares," the fraternity became something more. Although this so-called second order remained confined to the convent of San Damiano and thus could not roam free throughout the countryside in the same way that their male counterparts did, both groups reflected a diversity of membership that cast aside the usual socioeconomic boundaries of the day and both showed a radical commitment to a communal witness much like that of the earliest followers of Jesus in Acts.

If Francis had limited his ministry to those men who initially joined him as fellow friars and to the Poor Clares, then the movement he initiated might well have remained fairly short-lived. For various reasons, however, Francis founded a Third Order of Franciscans, comprised of many types of people—female and male, lay and ordained, poor and wealthy. They came with a desire for a simple and intentional life, and the suggestions he offered them (not yet a formal Rule) allowed them to make commitments as stewards of all God's gifts without confining themselves to the life of a friar or nun. Like Barnabas before them and Francis himself, these were not members of the church's "clergy" but became apostles of another kind. In a short time, not unlike that apostolic movement in Antioch, the followers of Francis first challenged and eventually overturned the feudal system of the day. Their simple, intentional life of stewardship touched all aspects of their lives and their environment. A good explanation of *why* can be found in those sayings that were collected throughout the life of Francis and eventually grouped together toward the end of his life, known collectively as the *Admonitions*.

There are twenty-eight *Admonitions* in all, together representing the apostolic principles of Francis. Like the message of Barnabas and Paul, Francis's life of holistic stewardship is grounded in his faith in Christ and the resurrection (Admonition 1), along with a realization that we ourselves struggle with evil (Admonition 2) and can only boast in the cross of Christ (Admonition 5), echoing our earlier statement that "God is God, so we don't have to be." Admonitions 3 and 4 focus on the need for obedience and humility, sounding not unlike the example of Barnabas as he eventually took the role of second to Paul. Subsequent admonitions focusing on love (9), patience (13), and peace (15), all show his concern for how we operate, and all are grounded clearly in the scriptures. What is most noticeable, however, is the emphasis on humility, as seen in the call to turn away from envy (8), the need to be poor in spirit (14 and 23), the challenge to allow oneself to be corrected (22), and the importance of compassionate service one to another (17–19). Reading through all the admonitions, there is absolutely no doubt that for Francis, to be a Christian steward is truly to be a steward of others, for all are blessed gifts of God (25–27). The final admonition brings things full circle, as Francis reminds his followers that all good gifts come from God, and we must store up these treasures in our hearts.

In this worldview, possessions have no meaning—even for those Third Order members who retained their jobs and social relationships—for in the end, all belongs to God and we are stewards only. Such a view enabled Francis to do what many Christians before and since would have found almost impossible: during the Crusades he crossed through enemy lines, met the Islamic sultan, and talked with him at length about God and faith. Where other Christians saw only enemies before them, Francis saw potential friends and fellow pilgrims who needed to know how much God cherished them. Is it any wonder, then, that Francis has since become known not only for his life of financial simplicity, but also for his love and stewardship of the environment, of animals, of the sick and needy, of all creation?

Despite the outpouring of admiration which in his own time made Francis a living saint and, in subsequent generations, the most beloved of Christian heroes, the fact remains that he has had his share of detractors, both in his own time and into our own. Contemporary critics spoke of his followers as indolent and lazy, begging instead of being productive members of medieval society. Others have suggested that his total commitment to "Lady Poverty" was something akin to masochism. Still others have questioned whether his choice to be poor and make poverty a virtue actually did lasting harm to those who had no choice about being destitute, who really needed a way out of poverty instead of a romanticizing of it.

Such critiques are certainly worthy of study, but what is important for our purposes here is not his focus on poverty but his focus on the rich treasure that is all around us, in one another, in our environment, and in every good gift that comes our way. For Francis, as for David and Barnabas, all things come from God, and so anything we give of ourselves—whether our possessions, our service, or our devotion—is simply a giving back with joy and thanksgiving. There have been ascetics throughout the ages, but their names have been relegated to the dust. The memory of Francis has endured through the ages not because he was poor, but because he was infinitely rich—rich in joy and faith and love. His lasting contribution lies in the call to those who would follow him to let go of all that enslaves us, to unclench our fists and open our hands, and to look beyond traditional distinctions and honor one another as gifts of God. Truly, here was a new Barnabas for a new age.

## who then is the faithful and wise steward?

Returning once more to Luke, we come to the key question of this chapter: *What does it mean to be a faithful steward?* As we have seen, the scriptures have much to say about possessions, as well as the need to look beyond them and not be seduced by a focus on possessions alone, as often happens in pledge drives or capital campaigns. We see this notion of holistic stewardship not only in the model of Barnabas, but also in a fascinating passage that deals with the specific question of distribution. In Acts 6, we are told:

> Now during those days, when the disciples were increasing in number, the Hellenists complained against the Hebrews because their widows were being neglected in the daily distribution of food. And the twelve called together the whole community of the disciples and said, "It is not right that we should neglect the word of God in order to wait on tables." (Acts 6:1–2)

The remarkable thing in this passage—indeed what is often passed over—is the fact that the apostles themselves appear to have failed in their job as chief stewards. As shown earlier, Barnabas and others brought their financial resources to the feet of the twelve, who then acted as overseers and managers to see that appropriate distribution was made and no one was left in need. And yet, in Acts 6, problems are occurring. What is the difference between Acts 2 and Acts 6? The difference lies in the recipients. That earliest community in Jerusalem was composed mainly of Jewish followers of a Jewish messiah—a fairly homogeneous group. They lacked the conflict of later Pauline communities, as evidenced in his letters, but they also lacked the diversity of those communities ("Jew and Greek, slave and free, male and female"). The diversity is just beginning to appear in Acts 6, as the newcomers are different from the regulars and are complaining that they are being treated differently.

What is the response of the twelve? They seem to distance themselves from the task and suggest instead that the people, implicitly the Hellenists, appoint seven individuals from among themselves—insiders in that particular relational network of newcomers—to respond to the complaints arising from within that group. Whatever positive light we put on the apostles' statement in 6.2, the fact remains that the twelve refused to engage personally in the work of distribution which they previously oversaw, a work that now moved into the hands of the newcomers themselves. God certainly blessed the work of those Hellenist newcomers and the church grew—but not the church in Jerusalem.

Indeed, in Acts 11:19–26, Luke goes on to show how those newcomers who had been scattered after Stephen's martyrdom (11:19; cf. 8:1–4) begin to proclaim the gospel *without hesitation* to Hellenists as well as to the Jews (11:20; cf. 6:1). The twelve appear to be confined by their own limits. They had commissioned the seven to a specific task—help bring about more equal distribution and thereby silence the dissenting Hellenists—and the latter had now fulfilled that task, albeit in a much broader sense than that probably envisioned by the twelve, acting as a catalyst for radical change to the entire existing system. Following the Council in Jerusalem in Acts 15, Peter and the rest of the twelve disappear from Luke's account altogether, as the newcomers—particularly Barnabas and Paul—take on the task of mission and ministry, of holistic stewardship.

What, then, does it mean to be a faithful and wise steward? Just ask our tour guides. For David, it meant recognizing that all good things come from God, and whatever we do or give is in thankful response. For Francis, it meant seeing the interconnectedness of all, and embracing a life rich in care and compassion for all those around us. And for Barnabas of Cyprus, to be a faithful and wise steward meant moving beyond conventional fears and biases and becoming an intentional agent of potential change, clear welcome, and generous spirit. The challenge of being a Barnabas in our own time, in our own situations, is what awaits us next on the journey.

# chapter three

# Suggested Route

*It is a shame when the money-raising boys get hold of so powerful a concept as stewardship and debase it into a way of increasing church income. Properly taught, the idea of stewardship can become a means of grace.*
—The Episcopalian's Dictionary (1974)

At the heart of this chapter is movement. We are called to move from an April 15th view of "church taxes" to a December 25th appreciation of joyful giving. We are called to move from being predictable to creative. We are called to move from a once-a-year spotlight on stewardship to a year-round timeframe. We are called to move from a purely financial focus to a more holistic approach, recognizing that it is not enough to meet the budget. No, the biggest challenge in moving forward in stewardship is not pledges but people. We are called to move to a place in our life together where we truly are stewards of all that God has given us, especially one another!

As we engage in this kind of movement, we face several obstacles. To illustrate this, I often ask groups to break up into pairs, with each person sitting back-to-back with his or her partner. One is facing the blackboard or posterboard, on which is revealed a picture of interconnected geometric shapes. That person must then tell the partner to recreate that exact picture, but remain back-to-back so as not to see the drawer's progress. Likewise, the drawer cannot turn around to see the image and cannot ask questions or respond verbally in any way, just listen, and draw.

The exercise is timed so that the pair has only sixty seconds to complete it, and often I walk about the room during that minute, attempting to distract all the various participants while they are in the midst of their task. Once 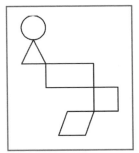 the sixty seconds is up, I invite all the various pairs to see how they did. As is probably obvious, there is a lot of laughter at this point, as each pair sees clearly how very difficult the communication of simple shapes really is. How much more the communication of a vision of stewardship! What are some of the obstacles to such communication?

First, there is the time limit itself. In the parish we face similar *time constraints* in the form of deadlines and competing events, especially for Gen Xers and Millennials, for whom time is far more precious than money. Schools and extracurricular activities vie with the parish for members' time, and churches do not drop people from the team if they miss a Sunday. Church leaders often spend so much time and effort talking about inconsequential issues, "majoring in the minors."

Then there is the obstacle of *one-way communication.* Only the person seeing the picture could talk, while the drawer could only listen and draw. This situation may seem contrived, but the fact is that one-way communication abounds in congregations. The greatest example of this is the sermon! Research has clearly shown that simply talking to people is the least effective form of communication, and yet this is exactly what a sermon is. I cannot begin to say how many times I thought I had preached one thing, only to have parishioners make clear to me in their after-service comments that something very different had been heard. Newsletters and bulletins reinforce a sense of unidirectional messaging, and even our websites are often passive and one-way in their format. I am not implying that we should cease preaching or stop sending out newsletters, but it is crucial that we see the potential obstacle to shared meaning that we ourselves set up when we do these things.

There is also the problem of *background noise,* as in the exercise when all the pairs are trying to do their work at the same time. The result is a bit of chaos, as several people are talking at once. Even so, in the parish we find many people often striving to convey a vision of steward-ship all at the same time, and often without any kind of coordination. The result can be very confusing and disconcerting.

And then there is the issue of *language* itself. How often the person speaking assumes that the listener knows exactly what is meant when a word or instruction is conveyed. This can be a deadly assumption. There are, of course, times when it is true. The speaker says to draw a circle and the listener draws a circle. The speaker says to draw a triangle and the listener draws a triangle. But then the speaker says to draw a rhombus (or a parallelogram, or perhaps a weird-shaped diamond thing!) and the listener has to figure out whatever that is and is paralyzed in the task or, worse, thinks he/she knows what it is and draws something completely different. I have said many times that Episcopalians speak in tongues far more than most other Christian groups, and we assume that members, not to mention visitors or newcomers, understand what is being said. The classic example of this is the typical Sunday announcements: "The ECW will meet in the narthex immediately following the postlude, while the vestry has a brief meeting scheduled in the nave, and the vergers and altar guild will join the sexton in the sacristy." How we love our Old English language!

Between that insider-speak and both the "pew aerobics" (stand/sit/kneel, sit/stand/kneel, sit/kneel/sit) and "book juggling" (Prayer Book, Hymnal, alternative songbook, bulletin, lectionary readings) that we impose on our participants, it is a wonder that a visitor ever comes back at all! And when we use other kinds of insider-speak to discuss such important matters as stewardship and giving, we simply add new layers of confusion. As the apostle Paul said in 1 Corinthians 14:19, "I would rather speak five words with my mind, in order to instruct others also, than ten thousand words in a tongue." He goes on to say that it is only the "immature" who use one-way communication or insider language and assume that shared meaning is being experienced. The mature Christian recognizes that talking is not the same as communicating. As James 1:19 says, "Be quick to listen, slow to speak, slow to anger."

Finally, there is the problem posed by *intentional distractions*. A more exotic word for this is "sabotage." In the exercise, I perform this act by going around to the various pairs talking to them about my car, the latest baseball scores, anything that will interrupt the speaker's ability to convey the information about what to draw. How realistic is it to consider that such sabotage is happening in the real world, in our congregations? Only the most naïve church member would not recognize how many times fellow members have sabotaged efforts in stewardship, evangelism, outreach—often doing so unconsciously. Church saboteurs are not necessarily bad or "the enemy," but that does not mean that we can afford to be naïve when it comes to their efforts and the likely disruption to effective communication that results from their actions.

Having considered all these obstacles, then, we can see that a simple ice-breaker exercise with geometric shapes really is not all that different from our real-world situations, as we try to communicate a strong vision of, and strategy for, holistic stewardship. It is imperative that we take into account every possible obstacle and assume nothing...except that our assumptions themselves are probably flawed.

---

### be a Barnabas!

Where, then, does that leave us? As shown in chapter two, we have a scriptural exemplar for what it means to be a model holistic steward in the character of Barnabas. Now, it is helpful to explore in practical terms what it might mean for us to "be a Barnabas" in our own time and context, not unlike Francis of Assisi or others in their contexts. The following, then, outlines a one- to two-year program of intentionality that can be adapted by any sized congregation. To help organize this exploration in a clear, easily remembered manner, the name "Barnabas" itself can be utilized as a mnemonic device, an acronym:

Begin with the big picture
Arrange structures strategically
Retain and recruit newcomers
Nurture fellow leaders and stewards
Ask for direction and support
Budget with vision
Analyze giving patterns
Specify a strategic pledging plan.

I am well aware that acronyms can often feel forced and artificial. A former colleague of mine once told me that he has a knee-jerk response to acronyms! Well, I certainly hope that such is not the case for you, but if it is, then feel free simply to ignore the fact that the following steps help form an acronym and just focus on the steps themselves. If, on the other hand, you do appreciate a memory-aid, then enjoy that as well!

## begin with the big picture

If we return to the geometric shapes exercise at the start of this chapter, we can say that one of the best ways to help someone else know how to draw the shapes is first to give them the big picture: "It is a series of geometric shapes all joined one to another. First shape, top left is a circle. . . ." For many of our members, stewardship is reduced solely to pledging; it is like focusing solely on the rhombus. We can get caught up in disagreements about that rhombus—about how to approach pledging—without first seeing where it fits within the big picture of a more holistic vision of stewardship, and how it fits with the other pieces that make up that big picture.

See Tool 1 in chapter four for a detailed outline summary of the Barnabas plan.

This is why, whenever a vestry or group of other congregational leaders ask me to visit and speak with them about stewardship, I do not begin with a presentation of the latest pledge program, but instead ask them a more foundational question: "Why does your church exist?" The response almost always involves either blank stares or something like, "We've been around for over one hundred years!" Their response suggests a misunderstanding of the question. After all, I am not asking *how long* their church has existed, but *why* it exists. This is not a superficial question, and is not unconnected to pledging and similar financial issues. After all, there are other groups that provide for individual and communal needs, and there are certainly wonderful churches of other traditions to which people can choose to belong. What, then, is the point of *this* church? What difference would it make to both the members and the surrounding community if it was not there? And, more to the point, why in the world should I give of my "time, talent, and treasure" to this congregation if I am not clear about its identity and its purpose?

See Tool 2 in chapter four for sample questions that could be used in a parish questionnaire.

Some church leaders will in response point out that they have a mission or vision statement. If asked to share it, however, they usually start looking in their vestry manual or church bulletin to find it. They may have worked hard to form that statement, but if they cannot immediately and enthusiastically share it, then I question how real and relevant it is to them. This is why it is crucial to find other ways to discuss identity, vision, and mission. But before we explore that, let me first be clear: I welcome vision statements and mission statements. I am all too aware, however, that such statements pose the danger of being either too vague to function as a specific marker of a particular congregation (after all, could not every Christian congregation, whatever its denominational affiliation, claim the statement "To know Christ and make Christ known"?), or too lengthy and detailed to be remembered at all (there are many full-page and even two-page mission statements!).

This is why the sacred bundle concept can complement and expand the good work of mission statements and vision statements, and perhaps take us further as church leaders. As mentioned in chapter one, the sacred bundle allows us to collect our individual stories into a common narrative. Although a well-crafted survey can be helpful, the approach of storytelling and open-ended questions can open up deeper understandings of corporate identity. A specific process can be used to help explore the church's identity and then discern the roles and goals of the parish in relation to it. That process includes the formation of a Heritage Commission to explore the history of the congregation, the formation of a Horizons Commission to consider mission and ministry possibilities that lie before the church, and a parishwide, weeks-long exploration of the sacred bundle.

FORM A HERITAGE COMMISSION

Such an ad hoc group can be commissioned by the vestry for three to nine months to study the history of the church and look for interesting patterns. Study begins with the group itself. Using the kinds of questions suggested below and in the sample questionnaire (Tool 2) as a guide, develop a one-page summary paper for every three- to five-year period in the church's life:

- What was its purpose in that period?

- Who were the leaders, clergy and lay? How did they lead?

- What resistance, if any, did they face? What obstacles were before the church?

- What turning points occurred during this period?

- What significant programs or buildings were created?

- If someone wrote a newspaper article about the church during this period, what would have been the headline? What key points would have been discussed?

Take this information and add to it more detailed oral histories in the form of recorded interviews with long-time members, as well as large givers of record. Why the latter? Simply put, we need to know why our top givers do give. Their remembrances and understandings of the church's identity can help us as we move forward later with the budgeting and pledging phases. We are usually happy to take their money but forget to ask for their input. In many ways, what is being discussed here is something like the first phase of an "Every Member Canvass," only instead of asking for money we are asking for information, which also means we are inviting greater participation and buy-in from our members. The same questions can be asked of all, with the end result being the creation by the Heritage Commission of a people and event timeline that will be presented as part of series of congregational discussions, to be outlined below.

However, in the meantime, note that the Heritage Commission is serving a crucial task and helping everyone in the parish recognize that we are stewards of our history and heritage. By making this group's work a key component in the larger holistic stewardship program, we are reminding all that where we are going is connected to where we have been before, and that even when we make critical changes in our identity, we can only do so appropriately if we comprehend what it is that we are changing. The Heritage Commission can help us celebrate our past, repent of certain aspects, and as the prophets of old said, *remember.*

In practical terms, the timeline can be only one result of the commission's work. Specific projects can be set forth, such as the creation of a book, perhaps self-published and then sold to parishioners and others in the community. If there are authors in the parish, this is a wonderful project in which to enlist them, and have the rector write an introduction. Another, even more directly useful tool could be a DVD or CD-ROM presentation of the church's history and current parish life, with links to the church's website and utilizing the oral histories and interviews of members. Whether it is done by tapping into the talents of a tech-savvy member, approaching a local college or school to see if this could be an academic project for some of their students, or paying a professional company to create it, a digital history can be extremely helpful, especially as a gift to newcomers who want to know more about the congregation.

This is by no means a tool for the young only. All Saints' is a parish in an age-restricted community where the average age of parishioners is seventy. Yet they thought it was worth hiring a company to produce an impressive digital profile of their church that was put onto business card-sized discs, thereby allowing members to give them away as a wonderful conversation piece to their friends. And because the initial debut of the card-disc was at the beginning of a capital campaign and pledge drive, its novelty intrigued members enough to go through the entire disc, discovering things that felt new to them about their own parish and more clearly understanding their budget needs, which were explained there in narrative form as part of the overall disc presentation.

Whatever the final tangible product, it should be remembered that the Heritage Commission's process of engaging parishioners is itself the crucial work, and the timeline that is created is a key component in understanding the big picture. This work is complemented by the work being simultaneously accomplished by another ad hoc group.

FORM A HORIZONS COMMISSION
Like the Heritage Commission, this group is appointed by the vestry for a limited time period to do study that is presented back to the leaders and the congregation. Unlike the Heritage Commission, the Horizons Commission's task is not to focus on parishioners themselves, but to do some research into the needs of the

surrounding community and to discover new possibilities of mission and ministry. This recognizes the fact that we are stewards of our social and physical environment, and the end result is a greater awareness of the impact our church can make in the lives of others. Specifically, the Horizons Commission members spend their three- to nine-month period consulting with various community leaders to understand better what is happening outside the church's walls. They speak with the Chamber of Commerce and local realtors to determine the changing demographics in their area: Which surrounding areas are growing? Who are the people moving there? What kind of materials does the Chamber or similar organizations send out? How well known is our church right now with the Chamber or with realtors, as they are often the first ones to whom people moving into town speak? These are some of the questions that the Horizons members can ask of these groups.

More than this, the Horizons team should approach local agencies and schools to determine their hopes and needs. Churches all too often equate outreach to the most obvious of needs, such as feeding programs or prison ministry. These are wonderful ministries and they need to be done, but outreach can also take the form of new modes of social involvement. For instance, we could buy a block of season tickets to the local high school drama club's plays and advertise in their program, saying something like this: "St. James' Episcopal Church Congratulates the Main Street High Players!" If we do this once, it will be a curiosity; if we make this part of our outreach for at least eighteen months, we will find that this part of the community begins to view us as a church interested in supporting them. We can similarly see if there is a need for a weekly lay-led service at the local nursing home, or find out the needs of the public library.

The Horizons Commission thus has the delightful job of determining how we can become a "church for the community," as the newspaper of one small city described the local, involved parish. What better description of stewardship of our community could there be? It can include specific recommendations to the vestry for advertising, for projects, and for newcomer recruitment *(see below)*, thereby complementing the work being done simultaneously by the Heritage Commission. The next step involves parish gatherings.

HOST A SERIES OF PARISH EVENTS

If possible, it is most advantageous to time the work of the Heritage and Horizons Commissions so that their findings are given to the vestry in December, perhaps in time for new vestry members to be on board. In this way, the parish leaders can be prepared to host a festive program for the whole parish early in the new year, perhaps as an Epiphany party (sometime around January 6). Such an event may include a potluck dinner or catered reception with a giant copy of the timeline spread across the walls of the parish hall, including key events, clergy, and lay leaders marked in color along the way. The timeline can be drawn in five-year segments on sheets of newsprint or posterboards, allowing for easy reading and for space for church members that very night to go up and use a different color marker to add to the timeline, perhaps putting the year that they came to the parish or adding some important event that is not already listed. In this way, everyone has some part in the creation of the timeline. Various pre-chosen speakers could relate stories about the different time periods, and the night could conclude with the clergy leading the people in the Litany of Thanksgiving for a Church (pages 578–579 in the *Book of Common Prayer*).

This Epiphany event stands as the kick-off to a themed year for the congregation: "A Year of Celebration: Looking Back and Looking Ahead." Members of both the Heritage and Horizon Commissions are reintroduced (having been formally commissioned in the liturgy at the time of their respective formations months before) and their work celebrated.

The Lenten season is a time of focus on the identity and mission of the congregation through a sharing of stories. Small-group tables are set up in the parish hall at a convenient time each week (Tuesday or Wednesday evenings, for example, or even Sunday mornings between services if necessary). For the first night, the priest invites all present to create something like a sacred bundle for the parish. Vestry members are each assigned a table, and church members fill in the open spots, each one bringing with him or her some kind of tangible token for the first session, an item that represents for that person the very essence of the church. Going around the table, each person shares a story about why they chose the specific item to represent the parish. For instance, a person might bring a loaf of bread and then explain to the rest of the small group how on his or her first day visiting the church, a loaf of bread was brought to the house later that same day as a sign of welcome and fellowship. One by one, items are presented and stories are told, until all the tables have finished. Then, the vestry person or someone assigned by him or her acts as the spokesperson for that particular table and brings forward to a central table all the items presented in their small group, summarizing the symbolism of each item.

For the next several sessions, the priest invites the tables to discuss the several common themes that have arisen from the collection of items, themes such as the importance of music for the church, or youth ministry, or hospitality. In other words, a list begins to be created of the key things that make up the essence of the parish at this time in its history. This is then compared and contrasted with the findings of the Heritage Commission's questionnaire, as church members discuss how the church's sacred bundle has changed or evolved since earlier times. They are also introduced in one session to the conclusions and recommendations of the Horizons Commission, and challenged to decide if there are things that need to be added intentionally to their mission and ministry, something to put into their sacred bundle that is not already present. Each session can conclude with the group as a whole in a time of prayer, such as Compline from the Prayer Book.

Taking the results of these sessions into the vestry meetings, the church leaders deliberate about one to three new programs or mission foci that can be initiated that year and what it would cost in money, space, time, and human resources to reach the goals. All this can be presented in liturgical fashion to the parish at Pentecost, right before people leave for summer vacations. Then, as seen in later sections below, this will tie in nicely with the budget and pledge campaign for that year, as well as with planned giving, and even a capital campaign if needed.

Thus, what is being said here is that before we can even think about choosing a pledge campaign program—focus on the rhombus—we must first outline the big picture and involve as many members as possible in the process of discerning who we are right now and what we believe we are called by God to do together. Once some kind of big picture is formed, it is possible to see how the time, talent, and treasure of the congregation as a whole actually supports or belies their bundle.

## arrange structures strategically

A prudent church member once asked me, "I am fully prepared to be a faithful steward, but how do I know that you and the vestry are being good stewards of what you receive from me?" This is a valid question... and a good challenge. As we just saw above, the clergy and lay leaders are the chief stewards of the parish, and as such, we are called to model the kind of radical holistic stewardship that we ask of our members. It is crucial, then, that we examine all the various structures we set up in the church, and determine if we are being wise and efficient in our use of them. Note that I said *all* the various structures, not just our financial structures. In other words, if a visitor examined our budget, as well as our calendar of events, our list of programs, and our use of human resources (paid and volunteer), what would she or he deduce about our core identity?

See Tool 3 in chapter four for important questions to ask about arranging structures strategically.

In chapter one, we looked at a large church—a congregation that boasts a million-plus dollar budget and significant staff, as well as a blue-ribbon K–8 day school on its property—that spoke of children and youth as a priority in their mission, an essential element of their sacred bundle, so to speak. I asked to see their budget, their list of programs, and their weekly calendar. After looking through their one million dollar budget, I raised the question of why they did not have a paid full-time youth minister. "Our budget for staff is full," they responded. They did indeed have quite a few clergy on staff, mostly focused on liturgy and pastoral care. Volunteers were assigned to youth work. Looking at their weekly calendar,

I pointed out that I did not see any time other than Sunday morning and every other Sunday afternoon reserved for youth activities. Again, the reply was that the time slots for the church facilities were filled by recovery programs, adult yoga, and committee meetings of one kind or another. If asked whether youth ministry is a vital part of their sacred bundle, I would confess that despite the leaders' comments about its importance, a quick study of their structures reveals that it truly is not.

This last comment is not meant to be disparaging of an incredibly impressive congregation and its otherwise visionary leaders. It simply means that, even as Jesus said that a tree is known by its fruits, so the essence of a church's identity and mission—its sacred bundle—is known by the structures it has in place. Again, these structures include the physical, financial, programmatic, and human resources of the congregation. The strategies in place for how these resources are utilized speaks volumes about the priorities of the parish, and can serve as a reality check against what members *think* their priorities are.

I am pleased to say that when I pointed out to the rector and vestry of the parish mentioned above the discrepancy between their claim about youth ministry's importance and the lack of support in their structures for that claim, they took the news to heart and asked themselves whether they really did want youth ministry to be a priority. They decided they did, and immediately took steps to make room in their budget for a full-time youth minister and program funds, and explored ways to turn underutilized space into an exclusively reserved youth house. Theirs is an experiment in progress, as they watch and see whether this is an item they do want to be a mission priority over a long time, but whatever the ultimate answer to that question turns out to be, the fact is that their practical realities are now consistent with their claims. Any congregation that wants to be serious about their identity and mission must be willing to follow that church's example and look at their strategic use—their stewardship—of the resources at their disposal.

One of the best ways that the congregational leaders can do this is to make use of some kind of a mutual ministry review at least once a year in order to explore how the ordained and lay leaders are spending their time and energy. This is not the same as a typical performance review, which usually is one-sided (the vestry reviewing the rector) and fairly black-and-white (these criteria were met and those were not). Rather, a mutual ministry review supposes that all the leaders are working together to reexamine their priorities and strategies for the sake of the overall mission. For this reason, it is probably most helpful for the review to be somewhat open-ended in its approach, much like the parish questionnaire mentioned earlier. This allows mutual conversation to occur rather than the unidirectional assessment that assumes more of a board of directors and CEO relationship between vestry and rector. Indeed, the parish priest is most effective when acting as the keeper of the "tribe's bundle," helping the lay leaders stay true to their priorities and not trying to step into the roles for which they, in turn, were elected.

---

See Tool 4 in chapter four for sample questions that could be part of a Mutual Ministry Review.

---

This is why it is helpful for the rector to share management of vestry meetings with the senior warden, the former focusing on the "big picture" themes and the latter running the subsection of the meeting dealing with specific action items and resolution. The priest must hold the lay leaders' feet to the fire, as it were, when it comes to making sure their leadership and stewardship decisions reflect what they agree are the key elements of their identity and mission. It also is crucial to prepare an agenda with suggested times and appoint a time manager to keep things on track. How many vestry members throughout the church have complained about three- or even four-hour meetings! This is unnecessary, and reflects a lack of concern with the stewardship of the members' time and talents. The time manager does not dictate when to stop a discussion, but calls attention to those points when it appears the group is moving off its schedule. This allows the priest to ask whether they wish to continue in that discussion, or appoint a committee to address the issues raised therein. In other words, an agenda prepared by the priest and wardens and sent out early, coupled with a time manager who keeps track of where they are during the meeting, helps focus the vestry on their stated priorities. All this can be accomplished only if the parties are fully prepared and comfortable with their respective roles.

---

## retain and recruit newcomers

One of the most important things I have learned from Barnabas in Acts is that he saw himself as a steward of newcomers, the Hellenists along with the Hebrew believers in general, and Paul in particular. Successful businesses today will often say that their greatest assets are their customers, but churches all too often forget to take such a view when it comes to the visitors in their midst. Earlier, we witnessed the modern equivalent of the Corinthian problem of speaking in tongues. To break out of our "insider" tendencies requires intentional efforts.

### TAKE THE VESTRY ON A FIELD TRIP
A good start is for the congregational leadership to evaluate the church from the standpoint of a visitor. One way of doing this is to take some time together to explore the following items, perhaps as the bulk of a vestry meeting. It is even better if you can invite an outsider, someone

whose feedback will be heard and respected, but who has fresh eyes with which to view everything. What should you assess on your "field trip"?

## The Yellow Pages

The expense is usually large, but it is still the most-used print advertising tool, so make every square inch work for you. Focus on the most basic information needed: church name, weekend service times (only good if you are sure they won't change anytime soon), phone number, street address (with any cross streets), website address, "childcare provided" if true, and a one-liner that encapsulates what you want strangers to know about your congregation. If yours is a smaller parish, the tagline might be: "Where Your Name is Known and Your Gifts Appreciated." A larger parish might say: "There is Something Here for You," or "Find Your Spiritual Home Here." Again, be brief but clear.

## Other Print Advertisements

Church members often like the idea of advertising in newspapers on the religion page. Unless you have a virtually unlimited budget for the church, however, this is probably not the best use of funds, for a couple of reasons. The first is that, in terms of generations, many Gen Xers and certainly most Millennials have no idea where the religion page even *is* in a newspaper. They receive their news electronically. The second reason is that the religion page is, almost by definition, an insider's section. Individuals looking there to find a church are most likely church members from another area who have moved into town and are searching for what is familiar to them. If they are already looking, they will most likely not stop at the newspaper, but look through the *Yellow Pages* or online.

No, for the substantial cost of newspaper ads, the same amount could be distributed among several other less obvious venues, all of which could be geared toward the target group to whom you are reaching out. For instance, if people are moving into the area, why not contact the local Chamber of Commerce or Welcome Wagon organization and take out an ad in their publication? This usually is printed annually (thus, you get more for your investment) and is something that newcomers to the area *want* to read from cover to cover. If the goal is to bring in more families with children and youth, consider paying the small amount required to advertise in their drama, concert, and athletics programs. Show your support for the students by not submitting the usual "sales pitch" ad. Instead, follow the 3-S principle: Keep it short, simple, and supportive, such as "St. James' Episcopal Church wishes the Alexander High Tigers a great season!"— followed only by the church phone number and website address, nothing more. And do not forget the end-of-year school yearbook. Parents will notice these ads if they are done on a consistent basis; even students will take notice. Similarly, if the goal is to reach out to a large retired community in town, then find out what they are reading and advertise there. Such intentional advertising is good stewardship of limited resources and excellent stewardship of people!

*The Church Website*
In this new century, it is clear that digital communication is becoming the primary means of exchanging ideas and finding information. It is also clear that internet technology demands of its users an ability to process lots of data in very small amounts of time. Thus, the home page of any church website is utterly crucial. In medieval times, a picture truly did convey a thousand words, and the digital home page does the same thing now. It does not

matter how much wonderful and detailed information can be found on subsequent pages if the home page does not immediately grab the first-time viewer's attention and offer a sense of welcome and assistance in a clear, attractive way. Show activity involving people of all ages. Do not simply put a picture of the outside of the church building on the front, especially with the door closed.

The question to ask with a website is, "How can we help viewers get excited about our church and what it offers? Again, the answer might well be found through the help of an outsider, either a newcomer who was turned on to your congregation because of the website, or a friend outside the church who will offer honest, insightful feedback. It also does not hurt to seek outside professional assistance in website development. This can be in the form of a free consultation with someone whose work you have observed and with which you have been impressed. Since, as with anything else in life, you often get what you pay for, it may be worth hiring a professional to put together the site. It is equally important that an ongoing website manager be used, usually someone inside or connected to the parish, in order to keep the site fresh and up-to-date, so as not to lose people's interest as they return to it later for further information. Care of the website is not unlike care of the physical facilities; people will notice if something begins to appear shoddy, tired-looking, or uncared for.

### The Phone Message

I always describe this as a congregation's most underutilized free advertising. You can make it as exciting and as welcoming as you want at no cost, besides a few minutes of time and some intentional concern for the caller/potential visitor. Above all else, remember that a church's phone message is primarily for outsiders. So, we should always lead off with an extraordinary welcome.

Instead of the usual, "You have reached St. John's Church. Our service times are as follows...," it is important to let people know that you are actually glad that they have called the church office, "Hello and welcome to St. John's Episcopal Church. We are so glad you called." Those few extra words can make all the difference in the world for someone. Offer clear directions, including cross streets. Share the weekend service times; do not worry about having to tell every weekday offering. Make it clear if childcare is provided. If an emergency number is given, make sure it is a number that someone will answer. Finally, end with a summary statement: "We have so many other things that we do as a church, we would love to share them with you when we see you." But make sure that this is truth in advertising.

*Signs*
Many church signs have been up long enough that they are rusted or fading. Like websites, physical signs that are never updated or changed quickly become invisible, not only to people driving by but even to the church leadership. Take a good, long look and see what is conveyed with your sign: Is it attractive, fresh in appearance, clear in what it says? Buy an alternative sign and switch them around from time to time to avoid the invisibility factor.

*Parking*
Most churches have reserved parking spaces for two groups of people: their clergy and persons with handicaps. While the latter is commendable, and indeed necessary, it is interesting to consider what would be expressed to outsiders and insiders alike if you had an equal number of spaces clearly marked for "First-Time Visitors." Think about this in purely logical terms. The presence of handicap spaces and accompanying ramps and walkways suggests that the church is open to, and perhaps already

has, individuals who are physically challenged. It is "handicap friendly." Similarly, the addition of an equal number of slots for first-timers would imply that the church is "visitor friendly" and considers them a priority.

## Facilities

Directions should be given for where to go. A directional marker or map near the first-timer parking spaces can help people find their way to the most crucial (for them) facilities, including the church, the parish hall, the nursery and youth rooms, and, of course, the restrooms. It is crucial that we use language easily discerned by visitors and avoid using names such as "Robertson Hall" or "St. Martha's Room." While insiders may know and deeply appreciate the significance of these names, to seekers they are merely confusing. It is far better to point in the direction of the "Parish Hall" and when visitors find it they learn that it is called "Robertson Hall." Also, the vestry should visit both the nursery and the youth room at least semi-annually. People love to donate sofas and toys and other items, but are they old and tattered, looking worn out? It does not matter how impressive our worship service is to a new family if the facilities for their children are not equally impressive. This is where it can be extremely helpful to ask a "mystery church shopper" to visit the church campus and give a full report.

## Ambassadors

Congregations with official greeters can embrace and extend this absolutely crucial ministry by renaming them and rethinking of them as "ambassadors." These ministers would do more than say "hello" to visitors as they enter. They would host a table outside in front of the church doors, symbolically and literally going out to reach any visitors.

*Worship*

If someone new comes to my house for dinner, I do not wait until the third course to introduce the person to the rest of the dinner party. No, I make all the necessary introductions before the meal begins, so that there will be no strangers at the table! So why do most worship leaders wait until the announcements following the Peace to welcome newcomers in their midst? These same worship leaders also choose to move right into the formal liturgy after processing up the aisle and singing the opening hymn; the implicit statement made week after week is that everyone knows exactly what is happening and needs no instruction. When I have questioned this kind of assumption, I often hear as a response that we need to protect the integrity and beauty of the liturgy. Well, forgive me if I paraphrase Jesus' retort in asserting that "liturgy was made for human beings, not human beings for liturgy."

In other words, much could be gained and, from my vantage point, nothing lost if the priest opened the spoken part of the service by saying something like the following: "Good morning. It is good to be here together this First Sunday of Advent. Do we have anyone here worshipping with us at St. James' Church for the first time? If so, please just raise your hand." *(Pause for hands to go up.)* "Thank you; we are delighted that you are with us. Please fill out a visitor card in the pew rack in front of you so that we can know you and be praying for you. Now, our service of Holy Eucharist continues on page 355 in the red *Book of Common Prayer.*"

Note what is being said here. It is not simply a nicety, it is theologically appropriate to recognize that our life together is the richer for having someone new among us, and to fail to recognize that gift is poor stewardship. It only takes a minute, but the entire liturgy is enhanced by knowing that all who are present, whether long-term members or first-time visitors, are there as a gift of God to one another, and as a hymn says, "strangers now are friends."

CREATE A NEWCOMER INTEGRATION RECORD

This involves a parish office file of one-page records on every newcomer or new family who comes to the church. The idea here is to follow up on the initial welcome and track people over time, "From First-Time Visitor to Fully Adopted Member." It is amazing to me how few congregations actually track the kind of information I am describing here, information that is invaluable if we want to bring new members into the parish family. The goal of tracking is not to report on how the newcomer is doing, but on how we as church leaders are doing in following up and responding to the needs of the newcomer.

---

See Tool 5 in chapter four for a sample Newcomer Integration Record.

---

We are stewards of each person, each individual life that intersects with our common life, and we must take seriously the steps that are needed to bring them along in a way that honors their needs and their gifts. I have been to too many churches where the first thing the visitor receives is a pledge card and an invitation to join the choir. I have seen many others where the leaders are so nervous about possibly scaring someone off that they take a totally passive approach and wait to see if visitors get involved on their own. The Newcomer Integration Record helps parishes find a way between these two extremes that will intentionally, but carefully, increase the odds that a visitor will want to return, get involved, and eventually become an active, pledging member.

## HAVE NEWCOMERS ATTEND AN "INVITATION-ONLY" EVENT

One vital step in the full integration of newcomers is an "invitation-only" event to which they are asked to come. A formal invitation from the vestry is accompanied by a handwritten note from the priest. The event itself is a reception scheduled before the pledge campaign, so that newcomers can learn how the church is organized and spends its money: "We don't want you to be confused when the upcoming pledge campaign occurs. We want you to know how we operate here." Any and all questions are answered. Thus, good stewardship is modeled as newcomers see how their potential pledges of money and time are used.

## INITIATE A "MEMBERSHIP MOMENT"

Make sure that your new members are formally recognized and blessed in a Sunday service. We Episcopalians do liturgy beautifully, so why not have a liturgy to show the transition of a newcomer into a new member? This is not the same as a Confirmation service, which focuses on a confirming of the vows made at one's baptism in the presence of a bishop who represents the universal Body of Christ, as well as a further infusion of the Spirit for the work of ministry. No, what is described here is a liturgy that can be done twice a year in the parish, marking a movement of newcomers to fully involved, active, pledging members of the church.

The rite itself is simple, and fits neatly within the overall liturgy of a Communion service, usually done around the Peace. The people who are recognized have already been thoroughly welcomed, have participated in an inquirers' class, and have made it clear that they wish to make this congregation their spiritual home. They wish to be pledging members of record, having attended the "invitation-only" event and learned about the leadership and stewardship of the parish itself (more will be said about this below). The pledge represents belonging, shared ministry, and the gratefulness of another precious child of God.

See Tool 6 in chapter four for a sample liturgy of welcome for new members.

Barnabas understood quite clearly that newcomers to the church are quite possibly the church's greatest assets, and he thereby intentionally reached out in welcome. Perhaps this is why Paul would later instruct the haughty Corinthians that the members of the body need each other and should not imagine it otherwise. A congregation that does not take newcomer incorporation seriously is not taking stewardship seriously.

## nurture fellow leaders and stewards

Barnabas not only welcomed Paul. He also put him to work, nurturing his obvious talents, helping him to be a leader in congregational work. For us, too, newcomer incorporation does not end with the welcoming.

This is why I always ask church leaders, "Are your 'leadership lenses' stuck at 20/80?" We all know the syndrome: 20 percent of the people do 80 percent of the work, and often with some amount of complaining. Yet, if the distribution of work is suddenly shifted, there is almost always an outcry from the ones who were doing the work for so long. The repercussions are many, including with pledges. It has been reported that the lowest rate of pledging units comes not from newcomers—who, if asked, will give—but from those who have been in the parish for two years or more but have not been fully incorporated and utilized. This is a no-win game—so the only answer is to change the nature of the game itself. This means stewardship of human resources involves a move toward leadership development, to be a Barnabas who looks for the Pauls around us who need to be nurtured and trained, not simply welcomed. How can this practically be done?

One simple way forward is to consider church events that are currently being done, and think of them as training opportunities for our future leaders. For every event, it is crucial that there are co-chairs, one a "veteran" who knows the ways of the church and the other a newer member who can learn the ropes from the more seasoned member. These co-chairs then contact the church office, which supplies several names of various people in the parish: some long-timers who have not necessarily helped recently, some who simply love to be involved, and some true newcomers, who can be asked to be "brownie buddies." By this term, I mean that these newcomers are asked simply to bring something for a single event. If they respond by saying how new they are, we can explain that we are a church family that does *not* follow a 20/80 principle. Once the event is over, the co-chairs make a point of sending written thank-you notes to all those who helped and perhaps calling the newcomer "brownie buddies." In this way, no one person or subgroup becomes responsible for everything that happens, which leads to burnout. Instead, we empower newcomers and help them become "insiders."

This is only one example of intentional nurturing of future leaders. In fact, it really starts when the existing leaders, the clergy and vestry, begin to consider who in the congregation have gifts that are not being utilized at present. This may find its beginning in vestry members praying through their parish directory each month. Even more, it may mean an email going out each week from the church office with the names of any newcomers who filled out a visitor card this week, so that vestry members can pray for those persons in their personal devotions. Imagine the surprised look on a newcomer's face when she introduces herself to a vestry member at coffee hour six weeks after first attending, and the vestry member says, "Oh, I've been praying for you." After it is explained, the newcomer realizes that she really is being valued from the first moment she entered. It is crucial, then, for vestry members to move from praying for existing members and newcomers to considering the following possible next steps or even more:

* Think now of who you would like to mentor.

* Consider how you can share what you have learned from your time in leadership.

* Make exit interviews standard procedure for volunteers and staff, as well as for wardens and vestry members.

* Host a "Vocations Fair" where parishioners are invited to have a booth in the parish hall and highlight what they do outside their church work, either in their work or their hobbies.

* Host a series of teaching events that are open to the public, something like "Teaching Tuesdays," on certain themes where your members, including newer members, can draw on their expertise. An example of this from one parish is a series they held on "Taking Care of Body and Spirit." Their speakers were all members who had been in the parish for nine months or less. One was a former Olympic athlete who spoke on honing your body. Another was a massage therapist who had just moved into town, and still another was a licensed healing touch practitioner. Yet another was a sleep-deprivation expert. The result was a successful series with many attendees from

outside the church, and a real appreciation of the gifts of these newer members.

One more thing should be said here before moving on. Part of our "church DNA" that we often neglect concerns our community involvement. As mentioned in chapter one, evangelism and outreach really are intertwined. This is more organically understood in the Church of England, as I learned when I asked a priest to tell me how many parishioners he had. His response startled me: "About twenty thousand people." "What?" I replied incredulously. Realizing the misunderstanding, he responded, "Oh, we have about one hundred thirty members in the church, but the parish is twenty thousand people." I was reminded that the Church of England considers a parish to be the geographical area around the church wherein all the people, unless they claim some other religious affiliation, are to be seen as parishioners for whom the church has responsibility. While there are certainly many problems that can arise from such a "state church" system, as I witnessed firsthand in my years in Britain, I also found that there is much for us to learn from a focus beyond our church walls.

This means helping our members think of their stewardship of time, talent, and treasure beyond the church walls. As one church sign boldly proclaimed:

---

### ST. PAUL'S EPISCOPAL CHURCH
*Rector:* The Rev. Graham Kincaid
*Ministers:* All the members!

---

This church has the right idea. A vital part of the work of the leaders of the congregations is to help members understand themselves as fellow ministers and stewards in all aspects of life, not just on Sunday mornings. As suggested by the "Vocations Fair" and "Teaching Tuesdays," we can help our newcomers and long-timers alike consider their gifts and how they are being used in their workplaces, classrooms, and neighborhoods. More than this, building on the recommendations of the Horizons Commission, the church as a whole can choose certain projects that break down the barriers that separate the church from its world. If we think of a pyramid of outreach possibilities, we can move from the first level of more obvious needs like Habitat for Humanity and food pantries, to a second level of connections with schools, libraries, hospitals, assisted living centers, and nursing homes. The thing is that outreach in these areas also often results in new members, as people see how much we as the church care about them. The third and final level of the outreach pyramid is global, when we are able to adopt a single project on the global stage each year to adopt and make our own.

The key here is for present leaders to make a priority of empowering future leaders. To nurture all the members in their use of time and talent, inside and outside the church walls, is very good stewardship indeed!

---

## ask for direction and support

One day, when I was a rector, I came into the parish office particularly distressed about something; I felt as if the weight of the world was on me. The parish secretary looked at me and said, "Oh, I didn't hear the news." "What news?" I grumbled. "The news that God resigned and you've been named the replacement!" The good news is that God most certainly has not resigned and neither I nor you have to take God's place. And yet all too often we operate as if we do! The missionary movement in Antioch sent forth Barnabas and Paul only after a time of intentional prayer. Although we are a church marked by "common prayer," the fact remains that all too often we embark on significant projects, stewardships drives, and capital campaigns after having done a lot of preparatory work but without first committing ourselves to prayer, to asking for direction and support from God.

Even as it is good stewardship for the vestry members to be praying regularly in their own time for church members and especially newcomers, it is also wise to call for the creation of a Prayer Task Force. This group can have more than one task. First, it meets regularly for intercessory prayer during the time in which the Heritage and Horizons Commissions are working, with both groups giving the Prayer Task Force specific needs to be prayed for. Members of the Task Force can also help lead Compline at the close of each sacred bundle session in Lent. In the months before the pledge campaign, the Prayer Task Force can again meet regularly for intercession, and also help compose a special collect or prayer to be used during services. All this helps us as church leaders remind ourselves as well as the congregation that ultimately it does not all come down to us. God is still God, so we do not have to be.

Likewise, just as it is important to seek God's help, it is also wise to obtain the counsel of those church leaders who came before us. The creation of a "Council of the Wise," comprised of former wardens and vestry members, can be highly beneficial. The council can meet regularly (quarterly or semiannually) with the clergy and current wardens to hear about plans, and to offer feedback and reflections. In this way, these former leaders are invited once more to become partners in leadership, which is also good stewardship of their gifts and experience.

## budget with vision and analyze giving patterns

Now we get to the specifics of money. First, before we speak of how to receive money "at the feet of the apostles," we need to consider what giving patterns we have already seen in times past. Earlier, we saw how important it is to make sure that we as church leaders are good and faithful stewards of all that is placed in our hands for the work of mission and ministry. We explored the notion that our essential identity and vision, our sacred bundle, is made real through the various structures of the church, including our facilities, programs, staffing, and budget. We can analyze the pledges and non-pledged contributions of record that have been given in previous years, so that we can better understand and possibly respond to any specific patterns we find. Let's take this step by step and see what we can learn from such an analysis.

See Tool 7 in chapter four for several sample pledge analysis forms.

The initial categories we want to consider are the more obvious: the numbers of pledging units and the dollars that come from them. It is most helpful to look at this, and the other figures, for at least a five-year period if not much longer. The longer the period that we can analyze, the better the sense we have of any long-term patterns. Besides pledging units, we also need to include categories for the numbers of NPGs, or non-pledged givers: those who, for whatever reason, refuse to go on record as pledging but whose own regularity of contributing is equivalent to a pledge. It would be wonderful to see them make a move to pledging but it is enough for our purposes here that we include them in our analysis. Then, it is interesting to track over time the percentage of pledges that were actually received in the end. In other words, if a total of $200,000 was pledged one year, and yet the actual pledged income received that year was only $180,000, we would say that 90 percent of the total pledges was received.

Having looked at the more obvious figures, we then move into specific areas of change, as we examine both lost and new pledges. First, we consider the number of contributors from the previous year who did not pledge in this year, and the amount of money that was lost because of this decrease. Similarly, we look at the number of new pledges this year and the dollars that came in because of those new pledges. We then consider both increased and decreased pledges from the previous year, and their subsequent dollar amounts. These areas of change are helpful to consider, but to be truly helpful, we should move into even more specific demographics of giving.

Three areas that are of particular interest are age, length of time in the parish, and primary service attended. Age should be no surprise, as we have already considered the importance of understanding generational differences in membership and stewardship. It should be remembered that appeals to "brand loyalty" in order to solicit or raise pledges from younger members of the congregation are, quite simply, futile. At least, this is a working assumption based on understandings of generational differences, but the crucial thing here is to test this assumption by analyzing the giving patterns of members by age groups. Furthermore, it is interesting to see not only how many members in each age category are giving, but also how much they are giving. We may find that there is some real commitment to give in a particular age group, but less ability to give at the same amount as another group—or, again, we may find ourselves surprised by our results. The only way to know is to put the figures down on paper.

Besides age/generation, it is also helpful to consider the length of time members have been attending the church and what effect, if any, that has on their giving patterns. It is largely assumed that the longer a person has been a part of a congregation, the more likely that person is to be a contributor of record and to give more generously. Again, it is important to test that assumption, and see if there are any surprises to be found. It is even more intriguing to cross-reference the age groups with length of time in the church and see if this sparks any "aha!" moments.

The demographic that focuses on the primary service attended by a giver allows us to explore the differences between the various "congregations within the congregation" that we often have in churches. The expectation here is not parity per se, but awareness of the different patterns.

While our analysis of contributions helps us understand our income, we still need to show our stewardship of financial resources in the way we budget our expenses. For this reason, it is prudent to appoint a very small Visionary Budget Task Force to assist the treasurer in setting up a modified zero-based and maximum-input budget. What do I mean? Thinking back to the vision work done by the leaders through the Heritage and Horizons Commissions and the sacred bundle, the budget team meets for three to nine months to ask all persons whose ministries and programs have some impact on the budget to say what they actually need. We speak of the importance of "pledging units," but "spending units" are equally crucial to the financial stewardship of the parish. Many businesses utilize a zero-based budget, where you start with a clean sheet and work from there based on the needs of the various departments. This would be a modified version of such a system. The so-called uncontrollable elements would first be examined, including property and utility costs and staff salaries, asking how the use of facilities and human resources fits with the overall goals of the sacred bundle for the parish. Then, all the program items can be considered, as the persons responsible for the various areas of mission and ministry show in written form an accounting of what they believe is needed to fulfill those areas.

Having already sought the congregation's input on the goals and roles associated with the church's sacred bundle, this next step allows the budget team to make specific recommendations to the leadership that are consistent with the earlier input, beginning from zero and plugging in what is needed or desired. Then the leadership can make the hard decisions that are required of any "tribal elders" and work with the budget team to create a narrative explanation of the proposed budget that shows how every area fits with the overall vision, thereby inviting maximum "buy-in" from the congregation. As noted above, that budget should reflect the sacred bundle in such a way that it becomes a practical version of a vision or mission statement. The budget should be able to "preach well"—the priest's job is to utilize this document in teaching the congregation about their shared mission and ministry. If someone wants to know the vision, the mission, the identity—the sacred bundle—of the church, the budget should be a good indicator.

### specify a strategic pledging plan

Having explored the big picture of identity and vision for the parish through the sacred bundle, evaluated newcomer incorporation and leadership development, and analyzed parish patterns of financial giving, it is now time to tackle the "rhombus" in that big picture—pledging! We begin where we left off, in the fall of the "Year of Celebration: Looking Back and Looking Ahead." It is one year after the initial formation of the Heritage and Horizons

Commissions, and several months after the Epiphany timeline event and the Lenten series on the sacred bundle. Pentecost provided an opportunity to give church members a first glimpse of the practical mission initiatives to be undertaken as a result of the previous months' exploration. Now it is time for the next step. As with any of the work already discussed, this step is actually a series of steps or actions, taken over a period of time and starting with the leaders.

CREATE A STEWARDSHIP STATEMENT

Actions speak louder than words, but the first action that needs to be taken involves words: a statement, in fact. I don't mean some vague "spiritual" statement with which anyone can agree but that ends up doing nothing. We all know of pageants where the contestants are asked what they would wish for, only to hear the answer, "World peace!" It sounds good, but there are no specifics, no real commitment to make world peace a reality. A big part of leadership is simply taking the lead. Jesus certainly did this. The apostles and Barnabas and Francis did this. So, too, before we can lay out a strategy for increasing financial giving in the parish, our clergy, lay leaders, "Council of the Wise," staff, commission members, and task force members all need to take the lead by creating an unambiguous stewardship statement that they can sign:

> We, the clergy and lay leaders of _____ Church,
> have unanimously and enthusiastically committed
> ourselves to stepping up our pledges this year,
> not simply to meet a budget, but to help us to
> go to new levels in our ministry and mission.
> We invite our fellow parishioners to join us!

Notice what this actually says. Barnabas gave freely and Paul called on his fellow believers to be "cheerful givers." It is important that our leaders are "unanimous and enthusiastic" in pledging and in choosing to "step up" their pledges. The stepping-up reflects commitment to the big picture that they have endorsed: "We believe in this vision and we are willing to demonstrate that through our increased pledges." The anonymity factor in pledging is not violated here; we do not need to know how much each leader gives or how much they step up that pledge. What is needed is the clear commitment they show individually and as a group to the "new levels in our ministry and mission."

I know this is not easy for some. In fact, having worked with many vestries and leadership teams on similar statements, I recall a particular group that invited me to spend a day working with them for the specific reason of creating a statement. When, however, I began to help them craft the words, a couple of members grew quite irate about saying that they would step up their financial giving. "Why can't we simply make a statement about the importance of giving time, talent, and treasure?" one asked. Another added, "Since it may offend newer members, why mention financial giving at all?"

Making a specific statement of commitment may indeed be a somewhat fearful, threatening task for the leadership, but the fact remains that leaders cannot ask others to do what they will not commit to do themselves. It certainly would have helped if they had first engaged in the kind of work we have already discussed above. In any case, a true turning point for a congregation in terms of their giving comes only when their leaders lead the way. For this reason, the commitment statement, once it is completed and signed, then needs to be framed and posted, preferably next to a framed photograph of the leadership team. It needs to be published in the newsletter and placed on the website. It also needs buy-in from the next levels of leadership, including the Council of the Wise, the Heritage and Horizons Commissions, the Visionary Budget Task Force, and all staff and other committee heads. The statement should find its way to each congregational leader and group in something of a ratification procedure, recognizing that inasmuch as all of our different leaders really are the chief stewards of a congregation, it all begins with them.

### CREATE AN ACTS COMMISSION

Of course, it does not end with the leaders. Sometime during the period when the Heritage and Horizons Commissions are first meeting, or soon thereafter, the clergy and lay leaders should form and publicly bless—appoint and anoint—an ACTS Commission. Why use the name ACTS? This is helpful for a few reasons. First, it takes us out of the dilemma of trying to get people excited to join a "pledge committee," since there is so much baggage that comes with the name. Second, it immediately suggests to people that whatever this is, it is somehow tied into the Acts of Apostles, a New Testament book full of action and growth and challenges and opportunities, as we saw last chapter. Third, it also ties in directly to the giving program that will be revealed below, and indirectly to the prayer group mentioned earlier, whose work will continue concurrently with the giving program.

See Tool 8 in chapter four for a checklist of the work of an ACTS Commission.

Members of the ACTS Commission receive their marching orders from the vestry or other delegating leaders, who share in detail what they have learned from the findings of the Heritage and Horizons Commissions. The other crucial interplay is between the ACTS

Commission and the Visionary Budget Task Force, as the latter provides their analysis of giving patterns with the group that will now incorporate that information into a year-round, personalized, multifaceted giving program. What would such a program look like?

## MAKE IT A YEAR-ROUND PROGRAM

For most congregations October is the church's version of April 15. For this reason, it is important to change the rules of the predictable pledge game by adopting a year-round approach. This does not mean that we suddenly start asking for money all the time, like some stereotypical televangelists, but it does mean utilizing the seasons of the church year to our advantage and making the annual pledge campaign simply one aspect of a larger strategic plan of giving. In that first autumn period, then, the ACTS Commission can do three things.

First, publicize the stewardship statement described above. "This is what your clergy and lay leaders have committed themselves to do. And for what reason? Because they are committed to the vision for the coming year that we heard about at Pentecost."

Second, just as a series of parish events focuses on the church's identity and vision in Lent, so the ACTS Commission can offer a fall series of small-group scripture studies based on the first nine chapters of the book of Acts. A study guide for eight sessions entitled *Acts: From Maintenance to Mission* is available for download free of charge from The Episcopal Network for Stewardship (TENS) website.[6] ACTS Commission members either lead the small groups or train others to do so, and then discuss the results.

Third, the ACTS Commission can announce that it will sponsor several one-shot teaching possibilities on money matters at different points in the church year. Utilizing the expertise of parishioners themselves or area experts who would like to tie in with the church, the ACTS Commission can have different members act as liaisons with these speakers and offer evening or weekend sessions on specific teachings ranging from tax and investment issues to educating our children in money matters. What this does is to let people know in the church and in the community that the ACTS Commission is committed to helping them become better stewards of all their financial resources, not simply to seeking income for the church. In this way, the ACTS Commission begins to be visible throughout the coming year, and as more than just the fundraising arm of the congregation.

## PERSONALIZE THE PLEDGE PROGRAM

Just as ACTS is an acronym for a specific formula for prayer—adoration, confession, thanksgiving, supplication—so it can also mark the way in which the commission can personalize the pledge program. We need to break down giving membership into categories, so that we do not utilize a one-size-fits-all approach.

---

See Tool 9 in chapter four for a summary of a personalized ACTS pledge program.

---

One way to do this is to think of four groups of parishioners that may be represented by the following categories spelling out the acronym ACTS: *A*postles, *C*ontributors, *T*eens and Children, and *S*eekers. How do we determine whose names are in each category? At the same time that we analyze giving patterns according to key demographics as outlined above, we also ask the ACTS Commission to work with the treasurer in determining how to place people in these ACTS categories. Let's take a closer look at what these terms mean and how we should approach each group.

*Apostles*

These persons are truly on board, full partners in ministry! Like Barnabas, they have a passion for God's work through the church and give accordingly. Although this group might well include some of the largest pledgers, they are not in this category because of the size of their pledge, and many large givers may not end up in the category. No, it is not *how much* is given, but *how committed* the giver is. In other words, whether what they give is small or great, these are the people who do not need to be given the same appeal that others receive. They understand what is in their sacred bundle (though they may not know that terminology until we utilize it) and they also understand the financial and other realities that the parish faces. To address them the same way that we address other, far less committed givers is insulting. Instead, we should:

Thank them!
Thank them!
Thank them again!
Ask for their input, their ideas.

Quite simply, this "A" group deserves a personal letter of thanks from the priest, as well as lunch or coffee to talk about the direction of the parish, not unlike the Council of the Wise discussed earlier. This group, especially if they are used to appeals to give more, needs to know how much they are appreciated and how valuable their ideas are. The priest can share the leadership's plans for the coming year, discuss possibilities of new and enhanced programs, ask for feedback on the efforts of the past year. Thus, input, not simply money, is being sought.

At the same time that they receive a direct, personal word from the clergy, it is important that they also receive a formal letter of appreciation from the ACTS Commission and vestry, written on church stationary and specific in its thanks. In other words, this is more than a form letter. It includes appreciation of the contributions of time and energy on the giver's part, recognizing that those who are committed in their financial giving are likely to be giving of themselves in several other ways as well. This letter is intended to be a "keeper," one that will be saved by the pledger.

---

See Tool 10 in chapter four for sample pledge letters for each of the four ACTS pledge groups.

---

Although such work on the part of the ACTS Commission members may seem onerous, in fact the number of parishioners who will fall into the "A" category is (unfortunately) small, and the payoff in terms of good feelings and renewed commitment all around is great. The only danger is in confusing big givers with committed givers, which is why we here utilize the term "Active." These people are indeed active in their mission and ministry, and in the congregation, and deserve to be recognized as such by the clergy and lay leaders.

*Contributors*
These persons understand that if you belong to an organization, you support that organization. This group makes up about 80 percent of all those pledging. So, send them a letter that does three things:

+ Acknowledges their support.

+ Explains the system, recognizing the different generations.

+ Invites them to join the vestry and "step up."

All too often, we "beat up" the congregation about the need to give more, instead of showing appreciation for what they are already doing. In this age of so many competing charities, people's gifts are indeed significant.

The letter should go on to "explain the system." In other words, if this majority of pledging parishioners does so partly because they think they understand the needs of the parish, it might be helpful to enlighten them further. A very brief *narrative budget* should be included with the letter, outlining how the budgetary expenses fit the sacred bundle with which, hopefully, they are already familiar from earlier in the year. It is also important in the letter itself to offer one or two "fast facts" to show the importance of their gift. For example, "You may be astonished to learn that our research shows that it takes 34 people to make our 10:30 am service on Sundays happen," or "Just to keep the doors open and have a bare minimum ministry for any given week costs about $_____." The beauty of this kind of reality check is that it is possible then to go on and remind the contributors that "We are committed to far more than just bare minimum ministry!" Here, it is helpful not to repeat the narrative budget but to reflect on the two or three initiatives that were fulfilled in the previous year and the two or three new initiatives that are proposed for the coming year, always in light of the commitments of the sacred bundle items. This shows a consistency of vision and mission, as well as briefly revealing what it means to "be a Barnabas" in terms of pledging.

Finally, it is crucial to reiterate what was said in the leadership stewardship statement: "Following the example of those earliest Christians in Acts, we the clergy and lay leaders have unanimously and enthusiastically committed ourselves to stepping up our pledges—not just to meet a budget but to help us grow to new levels in our mission and ministry." The crucial line is next: "We invite you to join us and do the same." This statement and accompanying invitation speak volumes, especially in light of the larger program of scripture study in Acts and the work of visionary budgeting that has occurred already.

*Teens and Children*

Most Episcopal congregations do not know how to help our youngest members of the church, children and youth, become Christian stewards. But the way forward is not overly difficult and involves the following steps.

* Evaluate our own work with young people.

* Offer creative teaching and training in stewardship.

* Schedule a session between youth and the vestry.

It all begins with looking seriously at the programs we already offer for children and youth. Perhaps what we need here is a report card, much like they receive regularly, to grade ourselves on our ministry for, and with, our younger members. Such a report card would reflect what we say is essential to us.

See Tool 11 in chapter four for a sample children's and youth ministries report card.

Note that youth and children's ministries have to be evaluated separately. All too often these two age groups are lumped together, despite the fact that there are considerable and fairly obvious differences in development and approach between the two groups. Note also that, as with newcomers, it is important to consider our "performance" in reaching out to, and working with, youth and children. It is an evaluative tool for *us*.

Also note that a prime opportunity for any congregation to deepen their work with children and youth is also one that is rarely utilized to its fullest extent: the acolyte program. This can be a ready-made group that can meet monthly, first for training in acolyte skills and then for training in other areas of church work and ministry, with the heads of ministries like lay readers, lay eucharistic ministers, altar guild, and ushers interacting with the acolytes and showing them how and why they do what they do. The acolytes can also schedule trips for fellowship and fun, and if the group is large enough, it can be subdivided into senior acolytes and junior acolytes, thereby respecting age differences. The major trip of the year, one for which they raise money and invest time and energy, could be the National Acolyte Festival held each October at the National Cathedral in Washington, D.C. What an opportunity to take a group that is only used to working on Sunday mornings, and helping it become something more.

It is crucial to engage the younger members in the governance and stewardship of the church, and to do this means meeting with them. This starts with the vestry, in a couple of ways. One key is for the clergy and lay leaders to invite the Sunday school teachers and youth workers to a meeting to discuss at length their observations and opinions. Then, the vestry needs to meet with the youth themselves, asking them to share their desires, questions, and concerns with the leadership. The youth of today are not the church of the future; they are, together with the adults, the church of today. Thus, it makes sense for a youth delegate to be elected to the vestry as a full voting member with a one-year renewable term. Young persons likewise should be invited to join the groups and guilds of the parish.

For the younger children, it is important for the vestry to make a "field trip" to their teaching programs and nursery on a Sunday. And it is so very important that their Christian education include teaching on money, possessions, and what it means to be stewards of God's gifts. This could include bringing in guests to speak about how they seek to be faithful stewards in God's creation: police, doctors, nurses, firefighters, teachers, bankers, businesspeople, scientists, and engineers. It could be exciting to promote a parents-children "meaning of money" session, where they are challenged to talk together about what money can and does mean. Many parents choose to "protect" their children from money concerns, which often translates as not speaking to them about money at all. Can we help them learn how to save their money, invest their lives, and partner with other Christians in the mission of the church? The statements about baptism in the *Book of Common Prayer* make it clear that "Holy Baptism is full initiation by water and the Holy Spirit into Christ's Body the Church" (BCP 298). Full incorporation means just that. Our children are fully incorporated members of the church, and we adults need to become more creative and intentional about recognizing them as such. This means training them in all aspects of parish life, and inviting them to give of what they have, even as their parents are being asked to do.

---

See Tool 10 in chapter four for a sample pledge letter to children and youth.

---

The sample letter to children and youth in the next chapter is one more important piece in this puzzle, followed up by time with them to have conversations about the governance and budget and mission of the parish.

*Seekers*
Much was said earlier about the importance of intentionally adopting our newcomers, and in no area of our common life is this more important than in stewardship. These newer members are not yet "insiders," and so it is important both to *educate* them and *empower* them. The "invitation-only" evening described above is an excellent opportunity to help explain how funds are used and the parish is governed. The process of personally inviting newer members is itself an important message that the parish values them and wants to involve them more fully.

Either in this setting or in individual time with the clergy, it is important to enable newer members to talk about their own experiences of money and church. Indeed, it can be very helpful for those seeking a spiritual home to unburden themselves of past obstacles they faced in feeling fully engaged in a parish: "All that last church ever did was ask for money!" Rather than hide from such a conversation, we can help these persons acknowledge their frustration about such experiences and then move forward in an honest, transparent manner.

As part of this transparency, we can share a narrative budget that explains the identity and vision of this parish, and show how and why monies are being used. Then, when the leaders express their commitment to step up their own pledges, it reinforces the fact that they are doing so not simply to meet a budget, but to support the exciting mission and ministry of their common life.

## ACTS DINNERS

Just as we host an "invitation-only" event for those seeking full inclusion in our extended family, it is helpful to host a subsequent dinner, or multiple "cottage meetings," for everyone in the parish to share in the message that the newcomers receive. Many churches already host events for their members, but they usually use them to talk about how awful the financial situation is and how much they need to meet the budget to save the church. And they rarely host a newcomer event first. Any events that we have need to fit what has been said above about the identity and vision, the mission and ministry, the sacred bundle of the congregation.

## NON-PLEDGING MEMBERS

All too often, clergy and lay leaders put a lot of emotional energy into worrying about those members who do not pledge, enough to warrant a few comments here. First, it is important to delineate between those non-pledgers who are in fact givers of record (making regular contributions via check or other identifiable means) and those for whom we have no record of giving at all. Regarding the former, it may be remembered that we marked a special category for "non-pledging givers" in the pledge analysis chart discussed above and in Tool 7 in chapter four. It might be useful at some point to approach these persons individually and learn why they choose to give but not pledge. The reasons may vary greatly, from philosophical objections to practical fears. In any case, this is a pastoral task, to be done in a relaxed and safe setting, a task that may yield some positive results both for the parish as a whole and, perhaps most importantly, for the giver—who just might have a story that needs to be shared.

Regarding those who are not on record as giving at all, it might be helpful to review the Newcomer Integration Record (discussed above and in Tool 5 in chapter four) on the individuals in question. This might reveal some ways in which we have not followed through in our incorporation of the person along the way. It may also be worth a quiet conversation at some point with the priest, as there may be personal dimensions that can be addressed. However, just as Jesus invited would-be disciples to join him in the journey, *but kept on moving forward whether they joined him or not,* so we must not expend too much energy here, but rather continue to keep the door open to greater participation. Again, this is what pledging is all about: not another financial cause to be supported, but participation in the mission and ministry of God in and through this parish. Pledging is participation! All are called, all are welcome no matter what, but not all may fully participate with their time, talents, and financial resources.

It is all too easy to focus only on pledges and thereby lose sight of the other avenues of funding ministry for a congregation. This is why it is important for parish leaders to consider the possible need and timing of both a capital campaign and planned giving. There are a number of organizations that can help parishes in these endeavors, most notably the Episcopal Church Foundation, but there are also things that needed to be said here about such work.

It has often been said that an annual pledge is "ordinary giving," a capital campaign "extraordinary giving," and a planned gift "ultimate giving." This can be helpful shorthand, but it needs to be unpacked a bit further. The annual pledge is grounded in work of discerning the identity and vision of the congregation.

See Tool 12 in chapter four for a sample pledge card that includes a variety of ways of giving.

By giving, we enter into the work of God in and through this parish. If we think of a participation pyramid, that pledge is the foundation, the base of the pyramid. The next level can be considered participation in the health and vitality of the parish in ways that build on the foundation but cannot be accomplished through the base alone. Some other means is required, which is why capital campaign giving is often called "extraordinary," because it literally meets needs that are not possible to meet through the "ordinary" means.

An effective capital campaign follows in its own way many of the steps already discussed. It begins with a discernment of needs on the capital or programmatic level, involving serious exploration on the part of the parish leadership into how certain projects fit and enhance the identity and vision of the congregation, its sacred bundle. Once the specific needs are clearly determined, along with the corresponding amounts of money required, then the so-called feasibility study is often undertaken. Quite simply, this is the time of securing "buy-in" from parishioners, as participation in the vision is expanded beyond the leadership. As capital campaign expert Glenn Holliman has often said, if this phase is executed correctly—meaning, if the leadership truly incorporates the rest of the congregation in the specified need and cost—then the next phase, the actual asking phase, is not only feasible, but relatively easy. Participation in input leads to participation in income. Any more detailed exploration of a capital campaign process goes beyond these pages. What is relevant here, however, is to recognize that such work is part of the overall stewardship strategy for the parish.

In terms of planned giving, the charge to the parish priest is right in the *Book of Common Prayer:*

> The Minister of the Congregation is directed to instruct the people, from time to time, about the duty of Christian parents to make prudent provision for the well-being of their families, and of all persons to make wills, while they are in health, arranging for the disposal of their temporal goods, not neglecting, if they are able, to leave bequests for religious and charitable uses. (BCP 445)

There really is no excuse for failing to make planned giving a priority in the parish! Like so much in life, however, this is considered by most clergy and lay leaders to be easier said than done, and usually takes a backseat to the seemingly urgent tasks already before them. The leaders of the Church of the Foolish will speak of how much they would like to devote some time to planned giving, but always find something else that grabs their attention.

What is so sad about the apparent disconnect between intention and reality is that there exists today an unprecedented transfer of wealth in the United States that will remain untapped by most churches. If we remember what was said earlier about the different generations, we will note that we are losing our elders, Brokaw's "greatest generation," in alarming numbers every day. Those who sacrificed and saved and who put considerable focus on brand loyalty are preparing to make their ultimate gifts to those institutions into which they have invested their heart and soul—and yet churches fail to acknowledge this fact in any visible way. More than this, the wealth they are ready to invest in the future is greater than ever before in history, and yet, again, churches appear unresponsive. When I recently sat down with a member of this "builder" generation and spoke with him about the ultimate gift he could make to the Episcopal Church, he smiled broadly and said, "I have been waiting twenty years for someone to approach me in this way. I love the church, but until now, no one has ever asked me." His words—"no one has ever asked me"—should haunt us in leadership, for when it comes to this kind of ultimate giving, the harvest truly is ripe.

What, then, can we do? The first step is to acknowledge our own nervousness about the issue. Let's face it: we would rather avoid any discussion about money or death. The combination can be particularly intimidating, which is ironic given that we speak of ourselves as a people who believe in resurrection. However, I have found that, our claims each Sunday in the Nicene Creed notwithstanding, most of us in the church live each day as if we believed in immortality, not life after death. For example, in attempting to discuss possible arrangements with the grown daughter of an elderly man in the hospital for what appeared clearly to be his final days, she responded happily that there was no need for such talk, for "Dad is so strong he will outlast all of us." I did not want to respond that such a statement is not only inaccurate, but also irresponsible. It is no kindness to put off important discussions about eternal things with those we love. And for the extended family that is the church to neglect such conversations points to a failure of nerve.

Perhaps I sound overly harsh with all this talk, but it is partly because of my own family circumstance. We always anticipated, because of an age difference and other health issues, that my mother would outlive my father. When she had a massive stroke on Easter morning several years ago, it was a complete shock to our entire family system, and made it clear to me how unprepared I was, indeed all of us were. There were so many things we had not discussed concerning her desires, and Dad's, about so many things. All the questions that would be thrown at us in those initial days following her stroke appeared overwhelming, precisely because we had not thought them through when it would have been much easier and less stressful to do so. At that time I was the rector of a congregation. I immediately decided to change the culture of silence that pervaded my own parish, and help families like mine have access to vital information that they need.

---

See Tool 13 in chapter four for a summary of gift planning options available today.

---

To be faithful stewards of God's gifts, then, means creating a twofold program, both pastoral and practical, for ultimate matters. On the pastoral level, it is helpful to provide a series of educational forums on issues of aging. Such a series could occur over four weeks, twice a year, with a coordinator and co-coordinator finding experts both inside and outside the congregation to offer free presentations, which would be open to all people in the surrounding community. This can become as much an outreach project to the community as our more traditional understandings of outreach. Topics for the presentations could include the continuum of healthcare options, from independent living through assisted living centers to nursing care facilities; legal issues surrounding medical decisions, such as a living will and durable power of attorney for healthcare; financial issues, such as the creation of a last will that reflects your personal values and how to set up power of attorney for financial decision-making; and support possibilities in relation to difficult medical realities like Alzheimer's and other forms of dementia, or home healthcare. There could be a fifth presentation specifically on funerary issues and final arrangements. For example, most people are unaware that there exist "burial societies" in most states throughout the country that provide a simple burial or cremation for a fraction of the cost charged by most funeral homes.

Throughout the series, by including experts from the community, who may or may not be parishioners, the parish can better interface with the surrounding community, and show these outside organizations that at least one church in the area is serious about the things that are of critical importance—and that we deal with such things as people of both faith and reason. Do not be surprised if you also attract some newcomers to the parish by opening up such a series, and even more if you decide to create or provide space for support groups like those mentioned above.

On the practical level, it is important right now to set up the necessary infrastructure to receive potential planned gifts and also to create a parish file for any "final matters" checklists that are provided for parishioners to utilize and store with the church, as well as in other relevant places (at home, with their adult children, perhaps with their attorney or family physician). Concerning the infrastructure for planned gifts, the Episcopal Church Foundation has created an entire manual entitled *Funding*

*Future Ministry,* which provides sample forms and letters that are necessary for an effective parish endowment structure. There is little sense in duplicating those fine efforts here. What is important is to review some crucial steps.

---

See Tool 14 in chapter four for an example of a resolution creating a parish endowment fund.

---

First, the vestry needs to create the actual fund into which planned gifts would go. This is done by way of a formal resolution, one that includes seemingly obvious but often neglected aspects such as the reason for the fund, the function and formation of a board to help oversee it, and guidelines for when and how the board is to operate. Beyond this, it is also important for policies to be formed regarding the acceptance of gifts. These gifts include simple bequests that are realized after a donor's death, but there are also other possible forms of contribution that can be made during a person's lifetime.

It is, then, important to qualify how the money invested in the fund can be spent and, perhaps even more importantly, how it cannot be spent. The endowment cannot take the place of the ongoing budget, and a planned gift does not supersede an annual pledge.

Again, what is recommended here is a multitiered program of financial giving in the congregation, one that will fund present and future mission and ministry, as visualized in the image of the funding pyramid on the next page. Note that each level is grounded in the one on which it stands, so that a capital campaign can hardly be described as successful if it is not built on the foundational piece of healthy annual pledging.

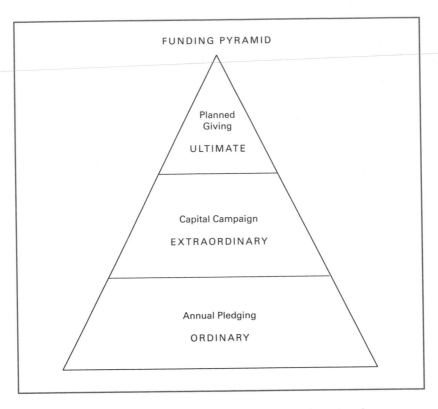

FUNDING PYRAMID

Planned
Giving

ULTIMATE

Capital Campaign

EXTRAORDINARY

Annual Pledging

ORDINARY

For those who inform the parish office that they have made such a planned gift, whatever its form or amount, it is important to acknowledge the gift by welcoming the donor into the newly created St. Swithin's (substitute your parish name) Legacy Society! Churches have long been slow at understanding the importance of appreciation and belonging. The Legacy Society allows us to accomplish both. The idea is to create a group to which every single person in the parish can belong and thereby make a lasting difference in the life of the church. The only way to do this is to make participation, not the level of the planned gift, the requirement for admission into the Legacy Society. "Charter member" status is bestowed on anyone who makes a planned gift (or lets it be known that they have already done so) in the initial year, which can be timed as part of the parish celebratory events listed earlier. A grand celebration for the Legacy Society closes out that year, with the names of all charter members unveiled on a permanently mounted plaque, along with a dinner or reception to show appreciation. As planned gifts continue to be made in the years to come, donors' names are added to the initial list. It is all-important that a letter of appreciation is also sent to the donor. By responding in these ways, we model not only a concern for the future, but gratefulness, too.

---

See Tool 15 in chapter four for a smaple letter of appreciation to donors for planned gifts.

---

## DON'T FORGET THE FOLKS OUTSIDE

I recall a confirmation service in which the bishop, standing in the entrance to the church immediately before the opening hymn, suddenly turned to face the street outside and made the sign of the cross, nice and bold. Smiling, he turned to me and said, "Always bless the town." It is easy to get so caught up with our internal needs in a parish that we forget the people outside, the community around us of which we are a part. Archbishop William Temple once said that the church is the only institution that exists primarily for the sake of those who are not yet members. God calls us to be stewards not just of one another, but of people outside our church's walls. Like evangelism, outreach is not *apart from* stewardship but *a part of* stewardship. So what does this look like?

Like the funding pyramid, in which the annual pledge is the base and built upon this foundation are other levels such as the extraordinary giving that is a capital campaign and the ultimate giving that is a planned gift, an outreach pyramid represents the various ways that we can reach out to those around us.

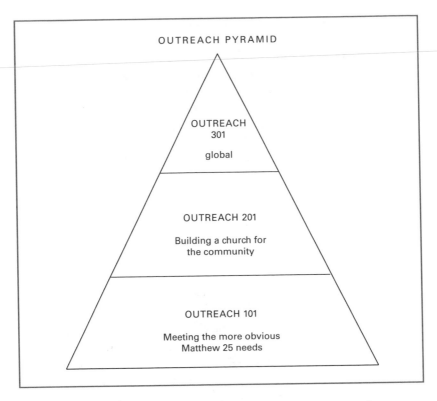

OUTREACH PYRAMID

OUTREACH
301

global

OUTREACH 201

Building a church for
the community

OUTREACH 101

Meeting the more obvious
Matthew 25 needs

As with the funding pyramid, the key here is to understand that we build on each base. As parishioners embrace opportunities to be stewards of the world around them by addressing the most obvious needs, they can then expand their understanding of outreach by finding ways to reach out to less obvious needs in the community, and then look to more global or environmental concerns as well.

The base of the pyramid consists of the more obvious forms of outreach that we usually think of when we hear the term: feeding the hungry, helping the poor, clothing the naked, visiting those in hospital and prison—in other words, the stuff of Matthew 25. I am speaking, of course, of the parable of the judgment of the nations as "sheep and goats." As followers of Jesus, we all know this parable, and understand in some way that we are called to help "the least of these my brethren." But we also cannot do everything. So, it is important that we as congregational leaders consider two or three projects that we can truly adopt for a year, and involve the parish not only financially but also with their time and talents. Building a Habitat for Humanity house, working with a local soup kitchen, running a food pantry—these are all worthwhile endeavors, and involve hard work if we are to do them well.

Denny and Leesa Bellesi's *The Kingdom Assignment* has been used in several Episcopal congregations to show another way of encouraging the kind of visionary outreach that is being suggested here. Their approach is to give parishioners "seed money" that they then are encouraged to "invest" in some kind of project to make a difference outside themselves. Every time, participants learn that there are opportunities all around them, and in the spirit of St. Francis of Assisi, to discover that "it is in giving that we receive."

It is only after we have helped our parishioners understand the importance of making a difference in the community in obvious ways that we expand our understanding of outreach to include the less obvious. By this, I am referring to the very things that have already been discussed throughout this chapter, namely supporting our local schools, offering "issues of aging" seminars open to the public, and creating support networks that are lacking in our area. Reiterating what was said earlier, if we can adopt a couple of these projects, then we are on our way to becoming a true church for the community.

It is also important, however, to make sure that we do not stop with local outreach, but look to the global picture as well. One helpful way of doing this is to hang on the wall of the parish hall a plaque that says "World Outreach" at the top and then has ten blank plates below it, one for each year in the coming decade. The rector and vestry choose one single global or environmental project that will fit in nicely with the parish's identity and vision, its sacred bundle, and focus on that project for the coming year. It can be helping a hospital in Gaza or working on a clean water program in Congo. In any case, the idea is that after some clear goals have been set for how to make a difference through that project, at its completion at year's end, the name of the project and the year are engraved on the first plate. The idea is that each subsequent year will bring on a new project, with the result that in a decade all the plates on the plaque will be filled in. This is a very visible, tangible way of helping us see ourselves as stewards of all creation, not simply our small portion of it.

---

## relax . . . and be transformed

If all that has been said in this chapter sounds over-whelming at first—"We just want to know how to increase our pledges!"—then take heart that the long-term health and vitality of the congregation and its people more than makes up for the effort involved in what has been outlined. Sure, we can simply do what we have always done, but that is the way of the Church of the Foolish.

Wise ones know that it is crucial to step out of the safety of the boat into the wind and the waves—as long as we keep our eyes on the Savior. The good news for us, as it has been for so many Christians through the centuries, is that we are not God. We can be a little nervous, or even a lot nervous, but let us not hold back from the hard work we have before us because of fear. We are called to be like Barnabas. This means, as we have seen here, that we:

Begin with the big picture
Arrange structures strategically
Retain and recruit newcomers
Nurture fellow leaders and stewards
Ask for direction and support
Budget with vision
Analyze giving patterns
Specify a strategic pledging plan.

Like the gospel parable of the sower and the seed, it is not our job to guarantee the results, only to plant the seed, water it, and watch it grow. Let us dare to leave the results to God! It is not only our methods that need to be transformed, but also our very selves. As Tom Gossen and Terry Parsons and so many other experts in the field have often said, stewardship is about conversion, not budgets and income. When we can allow ourselves to be converted—to be transformed—so that we understand that we are stewards of one another, stewards of the newcomers in our midst, stewards of our children and older members, stewards of our community, stewards of our facilities and budget and programs, stewards of the vision that God has given us, stewards of our church's own sacred bundle—then truly we will have become Barnabas!

# chapter four

# Tools for
# the Journey

*What Christians need from their churches and pastors is
the critical, evaluative tools to embrace positive change
and eschew negative change.* —Douglas C. Mohrmann

In the previous chapter we considered a way forward that
is both holistic and practical. To arrive at the intended
destination, however, more specifics are needed: specific
tools and specific resources. This chapter, therefore, represents our toolbox, containing outlines and sample formats
of the various materials that were described in narrative
form in chapter three. These tools are intended to be used
or adapted as needed by congregations in the development
of their own intentional stewardship work.

## Tool 1
### Barnabas Plan Summary

Much of what I propose in this book is based on the character of Barnabas from the book of Acts. Using his name as an acronym, we can lay out a comprehensive plan for holistic stewardship in the parish. A shorthand summary of the steps outlined in detail in the last chapter is as follows:

**B**egin with the big picture
+ How do we define our roles as vestry members and leaders in our church?
+ What was the vision of the church when it was founded?
+ How has that vision altered, evolved, or changed in the years since the founding? What can our timeline tell us?
+ How would we define the vision of the church right now? What is in our sacred bundle?

**A**rrange structures strategically
+ Do our structures line up with our defining principles and vision?

**R**etain and recruit newcomers
+ Target your advertising
+ Take a field trip of your communications system, your property, and your services
+ Be ambassadors and not simply greeters
+ Create an ongoing record of newcomers
+ Pray for newcomers
+ Create a "membership moment" and an "invitation-only" information event

Nurture fellow leaders and stewards
  * Empower others from early on
  * Think of those whom you would like to mentor
  * Consider how you can share what you have learned
  from your time in leadership
  * Make exit interviews standard procedure for
  volunteers and staff

Ask for direction and support
  * Pray
  * Seek the feedback and ideas from the Council of
  the Wise
  * Grade yourselves on key areas of ministry

Budget with vision and
Analyze giving patterns
  * Examine giving patterns in terms of age or
  generation, length of time involved in church,
  geographic area, service attended

Specify a strategic pledging plan
  * Break predictable timing patterns (October in
  church equals April 15 tax time!)
  * Move toward a year-round approach (There are
  reasons for the seasons!)
  * Consider your church's timeline; make the most of
  your heritage
  * Create a vestry stewardship statement, signed
  "unanimously and enthusiastically"
  * Personalize the pledge program

## Tool 2
## Parish Questionnaire

Although many congregations utilize surveys with easily marked 1 to 5 response sheets (for instance, 1 stands for "strongly disagree" and 5 for "strongly agree"), it might be more useful to obtain information through an open-ended questionnaire. The process requires a greater commitment of time and energy on the part of those reading the responses, but the results are worth it, since they invite a broad-based conversation.

The following questions represent a sampling of the kinds of questions that can be offered to the respondents. It is important to recognize here that less truly is more; too many questions will actually discourage response.

+ What are three things that we cannot afford to lose as we move forward?

+ What would you like to see happen at this church in the next five years?

+ If a newspaper article were written about the parish, what would you like it to say about our congregation?

+ What ministry needs are not being met?

+ What do you like most and least about our church?

+ What have been the most significant turning points or defining moments in this church's life?

+ How would you describe this church's relationship with the surrounding community?

- How would you describe this church's relationship with the diocese and the larger Episcopal Church?

- What would you tell a potential visitor who was looking for a church home about this congregation?

The goal here is clear: to invite maximum input, and hopefully maximum shared ownership, from our parishioners. This is why it might well be that the best way to make use of these questions is through an "every member canvass," with members actually being visited and interviewed.

# Tool 3
## Arranging Our Structures

In speaking about our essential core identity—our sacred bundle as defined in chapter one—it is all too easy to say what is important to us as a congregation, but fail to reflect that in our various structures. This is why, in our previous chapter, we spoke about the importance of arranging our structures strategically, asking some pertinent questions:

+ Does our use of the facilities...
+ Does our financial budget...
+ Does our choice of programs...
+ Does our understanding of lay and clergy roles...

> ...reflect our identity, our vision, our mission?
> ...reflect who we say we are in our essential core identity?
> ...reflect what we say are our priorities?

These structures can be illustrated visually in this diagram:

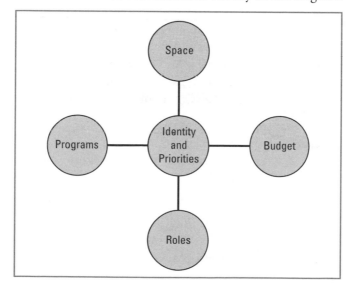

# Tool 4
## Mutual Ministry Review

Mutual ministry involves everyone considering ways that clergy and lay leaders together can work more fully and efficiently for the overall ministry in the congregation and the community. To this end, the following open-ended questions are intended to stimulate thoughtful preparation before the review and engaging discussion during the review. It is appropriate to bring written responses to these questions to the review, to make the most of that time together. And it should be noted that an outside facilitator is recommended for this process.

◆ What have we together accomplished in this year that we can celebrate? What is working well? How did we work toward our established goals?

◆ What are the things that the vestry especially appreciates about the priest's work this past year?

◆ What are some areas of needed improvement that the vestry could ask the priest to focus on in the coming year? Be specific: What specific requests would we make in the areas of preaching, teaching, administration, pastoral care, newcomer work, stewardship, leadership development?

◆ What are some areas of added support and shared leadership that the priest would like to ask of the vestry? Be specific: How can the vestry be of greater help in mutual ministry?

◆ What do we together believe the church needs to see and hear from the priest following this mutual ministry review? What do we want to communicate this Sunday to the rest of the congregation to encourage their enthusiastic participation in the common work of ministry?

♦ What specific goals and objectives can we set for the coming year? What action steps do we need to take to help achieve these goals? From whom else do we need to elicit participation and leadership?

♦ What additional questions, concerns, thanksgivings would we like to share with one another?

# Tool 5
## Newcomer Integration Record

In order to move from simply greeting newcomers to integrating them into the parish, it is crucial that we make a serious commitment to tracking—not tracking the newcomers, but tracking our progress in welcoming them. In this section a sample tracking form is provided that would first be filled out when a person initially visits, then kept in the church office and used as a checklist for each subsequent step of integration. Often the only paperwork involved with a newcomer is a visitor card. Some parishes then follow up with the delivery of a loaf of bread to the newcomer's home, and a call by the priest. With a checklist like the one that follows, these kinds of thoughtful acts become part of an intentional, regular process in which we hold ourselves accountable along the way.

Take note of the sequence. More things could be added, but this provides some basic ideas. The immediate need is for appreciation to be expressed for the visitor's presence in worship. This takes place in two ways: through a personal phone call or handwritten note by the priest and a formal letter on behalf of the vestry. The latter is important, because it lets the newcomer know that the lay leaders are also aware of, and concerned about, those who visit. Even as this letter is sent out from the office on Monday after the newcomer's visit, the office also sends an email to all the vestry members, informing them of the names of those first-time visitors, so that they may be praying for them throughout the next few weeks.

As discussed in the last chapter, the "invitation-only" information event is different from an inquirers' class, in that it focuses on the finances and organization of the parish. It is here that explanations are offered as to how and why money is spent, and pledging is discussed honestly. Having "brownie buddies" offers new members a chance to contribute their time and energy in a very simple way, by making something for an upcoming parish event.

---

### From First-Time Visitor to Fully Adopted Member

Full Name _____

Address _____

_____

Phone _____ home, work, cell *(circle one)*

Secondary Phone _____ home, work, cell *(circle one)*

E-mail _____

Names of household members & birthdays:

_____   _____

_____   _____

_____   _____

_____   _____

Anniversary or other special day:_____

☐  Clergy call in 48 hours          ☐  Formal letter in 72 hours

☐  Lunch with clergy                ☐  Invited to informational event

☐  Attended informational event     ☐  Added to vestry prayers

☐  "Brownie buddie"                 ☐  Filled out pledge card

☐  Inquirers' class                 ☐  Membership liturgy

☐  Added to directory               ☐  Confirmed or received

---

# Tool 6
## Liturgy of Welcome

As mentioned in chapter three, we are a liturgical people, so why do we not embrace this aspect of our DNA and utilize it when incorporating new members into our extended family? Such liturgical expressions can strengthen the commitment and communal ties of everyone present. It was said that this could be planned for twice a year, to allow newer members time to become comfortable with their own decisions about involvement. Optimum times for such a service might be the first Sunday after the Epiphany or the Sunday after All Saints', two days traditionally associated with new member incorporation through baptism.

♦   ♦   ♦   ♦   ♦

*New church members are seated in the front pews before the service. After the homily, the priest and representatives of both the vestry and the ambassador team stand at the front of the church. New members stand.*

*Priest*
Sisters and brothers in Christ, the mission of the church is to restore all people to unity with God and each other in Christ. We carry out this mission through both our prayers and our witness in words and actions. Together as a parish family, we welcome all who come to be with us, whether they are one-time visitors or newcomers seeking to find their ongoing place in a community of faith. And now we acknowledge these persons who have made known their desire to be included in the full and active life of this parish.

*Ambassador Team*
We present these persons to be recognized as fully adopted and active members of this church family.

*Priest*
Will you, as members of this parish, carry out the ministry of Christ in this congregation to the best of your ability?

*New Members*
I will, with God's help.

*Vestry Representative*
Will you bear witness to Christ wherever you may be?

*New Members*
I will, with God's help.

*Vestry Representative*
Will you take your place in the life, worship, and governance of the church, and offer your time, talent, and treasure to the work of God in this place?

*New Members*
I will, with God's help.

*The entire congregation stands.*

*Priest*
Will all of you witnessing these promises do all in your power to pray for, welcome, and support these new members as your brothers and sisters in Christ?

*Congregation*
We will, with God's help.

*Priest*
The new members will now lead us in proclaiming our common faith in the words of the Nicene Creed.

*New Members*
We believe in one God.

*All*
We believe in one God, the Father Almighty,
creator of heaven and earth...
...and life everlasting. Amen.

*Priest*
Let us pray for these persons as they take this new step
in their journey in Christ.

*Newcomer Committee Representative*
Gracious God, draw these new members ever closer to
you and strengthen them in their life in Christ. God, in
your mercy,

*Congregation*
Hear our prayer.

*Newcomer Committee Representative*
Help them to seek you and find you more deeply in this
community of faith and love. God, in your mercy,

*Congregation*
Hear our prayer.

*Newcomer Committee Representative*
Continue to reveal yourself to them through scripture
and the breaking of the bread. God, in your mercy,

*Congregation*
Hear our prayer.

*Newcomer Committee Representative*
Shine out through them, that their words and their
actions might draw others to the light of Christ. God, in
your mercy,

*Congregation*
Hear our prayer.

*Newcomer Committee Representative*
Give both to them and to us the grace to seek and offer forgiveness by the power of the Holy Spirit. God, in your mercy,

*Congregation*
Hear our prayer.

*Priest*
May God bless you and keep you, and may you find your spiritual home with these sisters and brothers in Christ.

*Congregation*
Amen.

*Priest*
Let us welcome our newest members.

*Congregation*
We welcome you in the name of Christ and offer you our prayers, our support, and our friendship. May your lives and ours be the richer for our common life in Christ.

*Priest*
The peace of Christ be with you all.

*Congregation*
And also with you.

*The service continues with the Peace and the Offertory, and a reception follows the service. During the reception, it is good to invite any of the new members who wish to speak to the rest of the congregation, sharing their experience of welcome and eventual incorporation.*

# Tool 7
## Pledge Analysis

As with the tracking tools for newcomers and young people, the reason behind the following charts is quite simple: to encourage greater awareness on the part of leadership and, thus, greater accountability.

The first chart focuses on basic information, namely the number of giving units and their pledged dollar amounts, as well as gains and losses in pledges, all over multiple years.

The second and third charts analyze respectively the number of giving units and their pledged dollars according to age, length of time at the church, and their primary service.

# PLEDGE ANALYSIS

|  | 2009 | 2010 | 2011 | 2012 | 2013 |
|---|---|---|---|---|---|
| # of pledging households | _____ | _____ | _____ | _____ | _____ |
| $ of pledging households | _____ | _____ | _____ | _____ | _____ |
| # non-pledging givers (NPGs) | _____ | _____ | _____ | _____ | _____ |
| $ of NPGs | _____ | _____ | _____ | _____ | _____ |
| Total $ giving | _____ | _____ | _____ | _____ | _____ |
| % of total pledges paid | _____ | _____ | _____ | _____ | _____ |

# lost from pledges last year that did not pledge this year _____

$ lost from pledges last year that did not pledge this year _____

# new pledges this year that did not pledge last year _____

$ new pledges this year that did not pledge last year _____

# increased pledges this year _____        $ increase _____

# decreased pledges this year _____        $ decrease _____

## PLEDGE ANALYSIS
### Number of Giving Units

| AGE | 2009 | 2010 | 2011 | 2012 | 2013 |
|---|---|---|---|---|---|
| under 20 | ___ | ___ | ___ | ___ | ___ |
| 20–29 | ___ | ___ | ___ | ___ | ___ |
| 30–39 | ___ | ___ | ___ | ___ | ___ |
| 40–49 | ___ | ___ | ___ | ___ | ___ |
| 50–59 | ___ | ___ | ___ | ___ | ___ |
| 60–69 | ___ | ___ | ___ | ___ | ___ |
| 70–79 | ___ | ___ | ___ | ___ | ___ |
| over 79 | ___ | ___ | ___ | ___ | ___ |

| LENGTH OF TIME IN CHURCH | 2009 | 2010 | 2011 | 2012 | 2013 |
|---|---|---|---|---|---|
| under 2 years | ___ | ___ | ___ | ___ | ___ |
| 2–5 years | ___ | ___ | ___ | ___ | ___ |
| 6–9 years | ___ | ___ | ___ | ___ | ___ |
| 10–14 years | ___ | ___ | ___ | ___ | ___ |
| 15–19 years | ___ | ___ | ___ | ___ | ___ |
| 20+ years | ___ | ___ | ___ | ___ | ___ |

| PRIMARY SERVICE ATTENDED | 2009 | 2010 | 2011 | 2012 | 2013 |
|---|---|---|---|---|---|
| Saturday evening | ___ | ___ | ___ | ___ | ___ |
| Sunday early morning | ___ | ___ | ___ | ___ | ___ |
| Sunday later morning | ___ | ___ | ___ | ___ | ___ |

# PLEDGE ANALYSIS
## Pledging Dollars

| AGE | 2009 | 2010 | 2011 | 2012 | 2013 |
|---|---|---|---|---|---|
| under 20 | ___ | ___ | ___ | ___ | ___ |
| 20–29 | ___ | ___ | ___ | ___ | ___ |
| 30–39 | ___ | ___ | ___ | ___ | ___ |
| 40–49 | ___ | ___ | ___ | ___ | ___ |
| 50–59 | ___ | ___ | ___ | ___ | ___ |
| 60–69 | ___ | ___ | ___ | ___ | ___ |
| 70–79 | ___ | ___ | ___ | ___ | ___ |
| over 79 | ___ | ___ | ___ | ___ | ___ |

| LENGTH OF TIME IN CHURCH | 2009 | 2010 | 2011 | 2012 | 2013 |
|---|---|---|---|---|---|
| under 2 years | ___ | ___ | ___ | ___ | ___ |
| 2–5 years | ___ | ___ | ___ | ___ | ___ |
| 6–9 years | ___ | ___ | ___ | ___ | ___ |
| 10–14 years | ___ | ___ | ___ | ___ | ___ |
| 15–19 years | ___ | ___ | ___ | ___ | ___ |
| 20+ years | ___ | ___ | ___ | ___ | ___ |

| PRIMARY SERVICE ATTENDED | 2009 | 2010 | 2011 | 2012 | 2013 |
|---|---|---|---|---|---|
| Saturday evening | ___ | ___ | ___ | ___ | ___ |
| Sunday early morning | ___ | ___ | ___ | ___ | ___ |
| Sunday later morning | ___ | ___ | ___ | ___ | ___ |

# Tool 8
## ACTS Commission Checklist

Returning to the ACTS Commission described in chapter three, the following checklist summarizes the work that needs to be done by that group in order to make the most of the financial pledge campaign.

STARTING NOW

- [ ] Consider and decide on the overall *theme* for the coming year.
- [ ] Draw up the vestry "step-up" stewardship statement for publication and framing.
- [ ] Begin tracking demographic data.
- [ ] Divide members into 4 categories: Apostles, Contributors, Teens and Children, Seekers. (This is done by whoever knows the pledge data— anonymity of individual pledges is still honored.)
- [ ] Begin drafting personal notes and formal letters to be sent.
- [ ] Plan "invitation-only" event for newer members.

FIVE OR SIX WEEKS BEFORE THE INGATHERING

- [ ] Send out personal invitations to members of the Seekers group.
- [ ] Finish preparing for "invitation-only" event.
- [ ] Put finishing touches on pledge cards, formal letters, and personal notes.

THREE WEEKS BEFORE THE INGATHERING

- [ ] Host "invitation-only" event for Seekers group and give out pledge cards at that event.
- [ ] Send formal letter on behalf of the vestry (with pledge card) to members in Contributors and Teens and Children groups.

- [ ] Send out different formal letter on behalf of the vestry (with pledge card) to members in the Apostles group.
- [ ] Priest or senior warden sends out a personal note to members in the Apostles group.
- [ ] Publish the vestry's "step-up" statement in the newsletter and on parish-wide email.

TWO WEEKS BEFORE THE INGATHERING
- [ ] Talk about the mailings from the previous week.
- [ ] Talk about the "invitation-only" event for newer members from the previous week.
- [ ] Place the framed vestry "step-up" stewardship statement in the parish hall.
- [ ] Publish a headline story about the theme for the coming year in the newsletter.

ONE WEEK BEFORE THE INGATHERING
- [ ] Announce the plans for next week's ingathering of pledges.
- [ ] Talk about the coming year's theme from the pulpit.
- [ ] Give clear directions about pledge cards in the newsletter and by email.
- [ ] Liturgically commission and bless the various groups and guilds of the church.

THE INGATHERING
- [ ] Have extra pledge cards ready for those who forgot to bring theirs.
- [ ] Frame the entire service around remembrance and expectation.
- [ ] Receive the pledge cards in a separate offering from the Offertory (perhaps after the sermon and before the Renewal of Baptismal Vows).

AS FOLLOW UP

☐ Immediately begin writing personal thank-you notes to those who pledged.

☐ On the weekend after the ingathering, announce the results and offer lots of public appreciation, not only for the pledgers, but also for the workers.

☐ Within two weeks, write personal cards to those who have a history of pledging but have not yet done so.

# Tool 9
## ACTS Pledge Plan Summary

The ACTS Pledge Plan, which was discussed in detail in the previous chapter, is summarized here for quick study. Again, the reason for having the treasurer or pledge chair partition church members into different categories is to help the ACTS Commission avoid the "one-letter-fits-all" tendency of most pledge campaigns by simultaneously honoring the desire for public anonymity of individual givers while personalizing the program. The following is a shorthand outline of the groupings.

### APOSTLES

These persons are truly on board with the vision and mission of the church. They do not need to be given the same appeal that others receive. Instead, we should:

+ Thank them!
+ Thank them!
+ And thank them again!
+ Ask for their input, their ideas. Their pledge will come!

### CONTRIBUTORS

These persons understand that you support an organization by paying your dues. So, send them a letter with three paragraphs:

+ Acknowledge their support.
+ Explain the system.
+ Invite them to join with the vestry and "step up" their pledge.

## TEENS AND CHILDREN

All too often, these younger members of the parish are completely overlooked in terms of stewardship. They are considered "the church of the future," but they, like we, are the church of the present! And we have a responsibility to:

- Recognize their presence and their value.
- Incorporate them more intentionally in the parish.
- Include them in leadership and decision-making.
- Invite their input and their pledge participation.

## SEEKERS

These are newer members who are not yet "insiders." So:

- Educate them.
- Empower them by asking them to an "invitation-only" event at which explanations are given as to how funds are used.

# Tool 10
## Sample Pledge Letters

These sample letters can be adapted to fit the different categories of givers in your congregations, based on the ACTS acronym discussed earlier: *Apostles, Contributors, Teens and Children, and Seekers.*

Regarding the letter to the truly committed givers in the parish, the Apostles, it is important to also have the priest send a personal note separate from this one, so that there are multiple ways in which these extraordinary individuals are reminded of the appreciation of the leaders.

---

### PLEDGE LETTER TO APOSTLES

Dear _____,

On behalf of the vestry and the congregation of the Church of the Epiphany, we would like to extend our heartfelt thanks to you for your dedication to the mission and ministry of this parish. We know that we do not have to explain to you that when we put forward the idea that "We Are Epiphany" we mean that Epiphany is a community of people contributing all that we can to each other and to God. You embody that idea. Your contributions to our health, vitality and growth, as well as your participation in _____ and as a member of _____, are a large part of what sustains our community of God's people.

As you know, this is an important time of change for Epiphany. In this time of transition, we are looking to raise awareness and the commitment level in our community. We ask you to pray with us as we bring the message "We Are Epiphany" to the congregation.

Enclosed are both a copy of our narrative budget for the upcoming year and a pledge card. Our ingathering of pledges for the upcoming year will be held at all services on the weekend of November _____.

Because of your dedication to and involvement in the life of Epiphany, we would like to ask you for your feedback. Attached are two questions that we hope you will take a few minutes to consider and jot down some responses. If you would be kind enough to do that and return the sheet to the church office or any member of the stewardship team (see below), we would greatly appreciate it.

With our thanks and blessings,
The ACTS Commission
_____, Chair

---

## PLEDGE LETTER TO CONTRIBUTORS

Dear _____,

On behalf of the vestry and congregation of the Church of the Epiphany, we thank you for your contributions to the mission and ministry of this parish. In this time of transition, it is vitally important that we all pull together as a community and affirm that, indeed, *We Are Epiphany.*

What do we mean when we say "We Are Epiphany"? In part, we mean that Epiphany is not just a building or a priest. Epiphany is a community of people, contributing all that we can to each other and to God. For example, you may be astonished to learn that our research shows that it takes 34 people to make our 10:30 a.m. service on Sundays happen—what an amazing gift! Perhaps you would be equally astonished to find that just to keep the doors open and have a bare minimum ministry for any given week costs $3,900.

*But as you know, we are committed to more than just bare minimum ministry!* We reach out to our community with projects like our participation in the Family Food Center and the Gift of the Magi food drive. With our new participation in the Justice and Outreach team, we have made a commitment to try to live the words of Jesus when he told us to love our neighbor. Educational opportunities for faith formation are also an important part of what we do, with offerings such as Education for Ministry for adults, and Popcorn Theology for young people. And we offer beautiful music in worship and praise to God with our new organ console and pipes, with other organ improvements still to come. These are just a few examples of our ministry, and there is so much more that calls to us in the future.

All of this takes money. For *all* of us, it is hard to know how much to pledge to the church. Some tithe, some do proportional giving—each of us must consider what is in our own hearts. Following the example of those earliest Christians in Acts, we the vestry, staff, clergy, and ACTS Commission have unanimously and enthusiastically committed ourselves to stepping up our pledges this year, not just to help meet a budget, but to help us to go to new levels in ministry and mission. *We invite you to join us and do the same!*

Enclosed are a copy of our narrative budget for 2009 and a pledge card. Our ingathering of pledges for 2009 will be held at all services on the weekend of November _____. Because *We Are Epiphany,* together we can create a healthy, vital, growing, and joyous congregation of God's people!

With our thanks and blessings,
The ACTS Commission
_____, Chair

## LETTER TO TEENS AND CHILDREN

As mentioned in the previous chapter, the one group in the parish that is often neglected in both decision-making and mission-funding is our youngest demographic, our youth and children. It is not because they are the "future of the church," but because they are fellow members right now, that they need to be invited to offer their input and, yes, their contribution.

---

### PLEDGE LETTER TO TEENS AND CHILDREN

Dear _____,

We sent a letter to your parents about Church of the Epiphany and what they can do to help the church next year, but we also wanted to send a letter to you! We are so happy that you are part of the church family, and that you come and worship God with us. Thanks for being with us and being part of our family!

Because you do different things at Epiphany than your parents do, and maybe see things differently than they do, we want to ask you a question. Is there anything else that you would like to see us do at church that we don't already do? If you have ideas for us—things that we could do, or things that you think the church should have—tell the rector or one of us on this ACTS Commission team (our names are at the bottom of this letter), or someone in the church office. If you need some help with that, maybe your parents can help. We're sure they would love to hear your ideas, too!

And talk with your parents about how much you might be able to give each week to make a difference for God through this church.

See you on Sundays!

With our thanks and blessings,
The ACTS Commission
_____, Chair

---

LETTER TO SEEKERS

The letter to members in the Seekers group is pure invitation. This is our intentional effort to adopt and incorporate them more fully into the extended family by letting them in on the family finances. Note that the following formal letter from the vestry must be matched by a personal invitation from the rector. This again shows that both the clergy and lay leaders are aware of the newcomer and eager for that newcomer to be more fully involved.

---

### PLEDGE LETTER TO SEEKERS

Dear _____,

We're so glad to have you as part of our church family at the Church of the Epiphany! Our annual stewardship campaign will soon be underway, and we realize that this is an important time to let you know about what we do here at Epiphany, how we spend our funds, and why we do what we do. As a newer member of Epiphany, we understand that all of this may not be clear to you.

So we would like to invite you to a special, invitation-only event, at our rector's home, to learn more about Epiphany! Please join us on Sunday, October _____ from 5:00 to 6:30 pm for wine and cheese and an explanation of how Epiphany works.

WHEN: Sunday, October ____
5:00 to 6:30 pm

WHERE: 1122 Main Street (at the SE corner of Church & Main)

WHAT: Cheese and drinks gathering
(Wine and non-alcoholic beverages are provided)

WHY: To learn more about Epiphany and get your questions answered!

*Child care will be provided at the church from 4:30 to 7:00 pm.*

Please plan to join us!

With our thanks and blessings,
The ACTS Commission
_____, Chair

---

# Tool 11
## Youth and Children's Ministry
## Report Card

We are stewards of our young people, and just as we need help to discern our progress with welcoming and integrating newcomers, so too we need to evaluate how we are doing in our work with children and youth.

The following "report card" is just such an evaluative tool. Beginning with the vestry and other leaders of the parish, it is helpful to offer this report card to several groups within the congregation, including parents and young people themselves. The results can then be put forward and decisions made about how best to proceed in improving this area of parish life and ministry.

---

**CHILDREN'S MINISTRY**
**(GRADES A–F)**

Use of facilities on Sundays for children's events \_\_\_\_\_

Use of facilities during the week for children's events \_\_\_\_\_

Involvement of clergy and paid staff \_\_\_\_\_

Involvement of volunteer workers \_\_\_\_\_

Training of volunteer workers for children's ministry \_\_\_\_\_

Priority of sexual misconduct training in parish \_\_\_\_\_

Quality of children's Sunday school program \_\_\_\_\_

Quality of Sunday school resources used \_\_\_\_\_

Quality of programs during the week for children \_\_\_\_\_

Adequacy of funding for children's programs \_\_\_\_\_

Input of children in the selection of programs \_\_\_\_\_

Involvement of children in worship and parish life \_\_\_\_\_

---

## YOUTH MINISTRY
### (GRADES A–F)

Use of facilities on Sundays for youth events _____

Use of facilities during the week for youth events _____

Involvement of clergy and paid staff _____

Involvement of volunteer workers _____

Training of volunteer workers for youth ministry _____

Quality of youth Sunday morning teaching program _____

Quality of youth weekend programs _____

Quality of resources used for youth ministry _____

Quality of programs during the week for youth _____

Adequacy of funding for youth programs _____

Input of youth in the selection of programs _____

Involvement of youth in worship and parish life _____

# Tool 12
## Sample Pledge Card

It is important to craft a pledge card that is a statement of faith and belonging for church members. The following represents one way of doing this for a particular context, but whatever stylistic form that is used, the crucial thing is to offer members a chance to be a Barnabas in whatever ways they have been taught throughout the year.

---

In thanksgiving for all that Christ has done in our life, I/we make the following pledge for the upcoming year, not simply to meet a budget, but to share in the work of God in and through this parish.
*(please check one and fill in amount)*

☐ Annually $_____   *or*   ☐ Monthly $_____   *or*   ☐ Weekly $_____

- - - - - - - - - - - - - - - - - - - - - - - - - - - - - - - - - - - - - - - - - - - -

I/we believe that our sanctuary is a vital part of our living heritage and I/we support the necessary capital improvements and renovations as well as the long-term need of a capital endowment. I/we wish to become a founding member of the St. Stephen's Heritage Society by making the following commitment over and above my/our regular pledge *(check one)*:

    ☐ Patron ($1,000 or more)   $_____
    ☐ Friend ($500–$999)      $_____
    ☐ Member ($50–$499)      $_____

- - - - - - - - - - - - - - - - - - - - - - - - - - - - - - - - - - - - - - - - - - - -

Please also note the following ways in which I/we pledge my/our time and talents to the church's work:

_____

_____

- - - - - - - - - - - - - - - - - - - - - - - - - - - - - - - - - - - - - - - - - - - -

☐ I/we have also made a planned gift to the Heritage Fund in my/our will and/or estate.

---

# Tool 13
## Gift Planning Options

It is good stewardship for congregational members to learn of their own options for planning their ultimate financial gift. Wills and bequests are only one piece of it, and while it is not possible here to go into detail about the various options, it is helpful to list some of them and invite individuals to explore them further.

IMMEDIATE GIFTS
* Large and small cash gifts

* Real estate properties
  *The gift must be, of course, free of mortgages and readily marketable.*

* Stocks, bonds, mutual funds, and other appreciated securities
  *It is helpful to know that a tax deduction for the donor can be based on the full market value of the securities on the date of the transfer.*

* Other assets and personal property
  *Whatever the nature of the gift (automobile, jewels), the donor's attorneys can create a "deed of gift" to determine the value on the date of transfer.*

DEFERRED GIFTS
* Wills and bequests

* Life insurance
  *"Whole life insurance" can be donated at the cash value of the policy at the time of donation.*

+ Charitable Gift Annuities
  *The donor receives from the receiving organization fixed annuity income payments until the time of death in return for the gift which is given.*

+ Pooled Income Fund
  *The donor contributes to a pooled fund that pays out income for the life of the donor or beneficiary.*

+ Charitable Remainder Trusts
  *A trust is founded that establishes the trustee while also providing income payments for the donor.*

+ Charitable Lead Trusts
  *A trust is constructed for a term of years, as a donor temporarily places assets with the organization.*

+ Life Estate Gift
  *A home may be left to the church now instead of at death while the donor continues to live there.*

# Tool 14
## Sample Vestry Resolution
## for Creating an Endowment

The important work of creating a parish endowment can seem daunting at first. The following represents a sample vestry resolution for creating such an endowment, and can be adapted in whatever ways are needed for your congregation's specific context.

---

### PLAN OF OPERATION

**1.   The Heritage Endowment Fund Board**

The BOARD shall consist of six members, all of whom shall be members in good standing of St. Stephen's Episcopal Church; they shall be nominated by the Vestry and voted to the BOARD by the parishioners at the Annual Parish Meeting. Additionally, the Rector and Senior Warden shall be ex-officio, non-voting members of the BOARD. Except as herein limited, the term of each member shall be three (3) years. Upon adoption of this resolution, two (2) members shall be elected for a term of one (1) year, two (2) members for a term of two (2) years, and two (2) members for a term of three (3) years. Thereafter, on an annual basis, the Vestry shall nominate potential members, and parishioners shall elect the necessary number for a term of three years. After a lapse of one (1) year, former BOARD members may be re-elected. In the event of a vacancy on the BOARD, the Vestry shall appoint a member to complete the unfulfilled term. At the next Annual Parish Meeting, a full-term replacement BOARD member will be elected as above.

The HERITAGE ENDOWMENT FUND BOARD shall meet at least quarterly, or more frequently as deemed by it in the best interest of the FUND.

A quorum shall consist of four (4) members. The affirmative vote of four (4) members shall be necessary to carry any motion of resolution.

The BOARD shall elect from its membership a Chairperson and a Secretary. The Chairperson, or member designated by the Chairperson, shall preside at all BOARD meetings.

---

The Secretary shall maintain complete and accurate minutes of all meetings of the BOARD and supply a copy thereof to each member of the BOARD. Each member shall keep a complete set of minutes to be delivered to his or her successor. The Secretary shall also supply a copy of the minutes to the Vestry in a timely manner.

The Treasurer of the Parish shall maintain complete and accurate books of account for the FUND. At the discretion of the Vestry, the books may be audited annually by a certified public accountant or other qualified person. Such person shall not be a member of the Vestry or BOARD.

The BOARD shall report on a quarterly basis to the Vestry and, at each annual meeting of the congregation, shall render a full and complete account of the administration of the FUND during the previous year.

The BOARD, at the expense of the FUND, may provide for such professional counseling on investments or legal matters as it deems to be in the best interest of the FUND.

Members of the HERITAGE ENDOWMENT FUND BOARD shall be liable for any acts of omissions committed by them (including losses which may be incurred upon investments of assets of the FUND) only to the extent that such acts or omissions were not in good faith or involved intentional misconduct. Each member shall be liable only for his or her own intentional misconduct or for his or her own acts or omissions not in good faith, and shall not be liable for the acts or omissions of any other members. No member shall engage in any self-dealing or transactions with the FUND in which the member has direct or indirect financial interest, and shall at all times refrain from any conduct in which his or her personal interests would conflict with the interest of the FUND.

All assets are to be held in the name of THE HERITAGE ENDOWMENT FUND OF ST. STEPHEN'S EPISCOPAL CHURCH. Actions to hold, sell, exchange, rent, lease, transfer, convert, invest, reinvest, and all other respects to manage and control the assets of the FUND, including stocks, bonds, debentures, mortgages, notes, warrants of other securities, as in their judgment and discretion they deem wise and prudent, are to be made by a delegated member of the BOARD.

**2.    Acceptance of gifts to the Heritage Fund**
The BOARD will establish a gift review process through which the decision is made whether a gift shall be accepted. If a gift of property other than cash

or publicly traded securities is offered to the PARISH, there will be conducted a careful review to determine whether the best interest of the congregation is served by accepting or rejecting the gift. Guidelines for conducting such a review shall be incorporated in the Gift Review Policy.

**3.    Distributions from the Heritage Fund**
It is the intent of this resolution that the FUND shall be managed as a true endowment employing the restriction that the principal shall not be invaded; however, distributions fom the FUND shall be made utilizing a Total Return Policy that incorporates a designated percentage of the corpus that will be available for expenditure annually. The BOARD shall formulate a policy defining the spending rules and protocols, with the approval of the Vestry, which will provide for the withdrawal and use of funds consistent with the stated purposes of the FUND as defined in the first section of this resolution.

No portion of the principal amount of the FUND shall be "borrowed," including any "temporary usage" for other parish needs.

**4.    Amendment of these Resolutions**
Any amendment to these Resolutions shall be adopted by a vote of at least two-thirds (2/3) of the membership of the Vestry at a regularly scheduled meeting or at a special meeting called specifically for the purpose of amending these Resolutions.

**5.    Disposition or transfer of FUND**
In the event the PARISH ceases to exist, whether through merger, dissolution, or some other event, disposition or transfer of the FUND shall be at the discretion of the Vestry in conformity with the approved congregational constitution and in consultation with the Bishop of the Diocese.

The foregoing Resolutions are hereby ADOPTED by the Vestry on this _____ day of _____, 20_____ at St. Stephen's Episcopal Church.

# Tool 15
## Sample Legacy Society
## Thank You Letter

Whatever name we give to it, the parish legacy society is the vehicle for making possible planned gifts for capital and extraordinary projects. For most parishioners, this can become their ultimate gift, whatever its size, and it is therefore imperative to recognize every person who makes such a planned gift through immediate membership in the legacy society.

---

Dear _____:

*O gracious God, grant that, by the prayers and labors of your holy Church, others may be brought to know you and worship you. Amen.*

We recently were notified that you have made a Planned Gift for St. Philip the Evangelist Church. What a wonderful mark of your commitment to the work of God in and through that community! Your legacy gift will help continue the good work of ministry and mission in that place for many years to come.

With that in mind, we also happily inform you of your immediate inclusion in the St. Philip's Legacy Society. As noted in issues of the parish newsletter, this society has been established precisely to honor the vision and generosity of those who are creating a lasting legacy in the parish. At a point later in the year, we hope to host an invitation-only event for all members of the St. Philip's Legacy Society, all those who have made lasting gifts to the parish even as you have. We will inform you of that event as the time comes closer.

Again, on behalf of the entire parish family, we thank you for your Planned Gift to St. Philip's, and look forward to meeting with you in person in the coming year.

Faithfully,

The Board of the St. Philip's Legacy Society
_____, Chair

---

This chapter has been intended to serve as a kind of toolbox, offering more specific examples of programs, processes, and forms discussed in the previous chapter. However, it is important to reiterate that we have only scratched the surface with what is included here. The fact is that there are indeed many other tools out there for your congregation to use. This is why I would recommend exploring the various books and organizations listed in the Resource section at the end of this book.

In the last analysis, of course, the tools are only truly helpful if they are utilized to support the kind of passionate and holistic vision that has been discussed throughout these pages. Barnabas had land and money to draw upon as he presented himself to the twelve for the first time. But much more important is the fact that Barnabas obviously had a heart for God and a heart for the people around him, whatever their background and their reputation. This "son of encouragement" is a bold example of how we are called by Jesus to be witnesses, ambassadors to the world around us, starting right where we are in our journey but never getting stuck in that one place. Barnabas is a happy example of how we are called to be stewards of one another and all those we meet, and the fact that he used the gifts he had at his disposal to make a mark in the world should spur us on to find whatever tools we need and then use them. The tools really are there; let us hear the summons of Christ to work once more.

chapter five

# The Destination

*Stewardship and the economics of God, like faith, cannot be taught, but they can be caught, nurtured, and lived into. And that is the ever present challenge before us.*
—John H. Westerhoff

Who has not heard that familiar question from the mouths of passengers on a journey: "Are we there yet?" For the driver, it is incredibly frustrating to hear, yet at the same time it is an understandable question. After all, the journey can be long, and for those not in the driver's seat, it is difficult to be told, "Be patient." Well aware of my own impatience as a child on family vacations, my father responded by giving me the important position of navigator, utilizing a map marked with the intended route to convey both our present position and the next best point where we should stop for refueling the car or ourselves. I thereby went from being a passive passenger to an active partner in the journey.

In a similar way, this book has been intended to serve as something of a roadmap for those interested in the health and vitality of their churches. It is less about an easy-to-reach financial goal and more about active and intentional participation in the journey itself. As said from the start, there is no "get rich quick" scheme for congregations who want only to balance their budget. Instead, this map is likewise an invitation to be transformed, to live into the role of Christ's holistic stewards and ambassadors as we chart a new course for the twenty-first century. The good news is that we will find, as did Barnabas and so many others like him, that God is with us in this journey. Like those two worried, weighed-down disciples on the road to Emmaus, if we keep our eyes and hearts open, we will find both encouragement and challenge from the One who walks beside us. We will be able to echo the words of the Prayer Book: "Be our companion in the way, kindle our hearts, and awaken hope."

---

## transformed churches

So what, then, does the destination look like? It is a congregation that is clear about its identity and its priorities. It is an extended family in which every member, from the long-timer to the newcomer, is involved in the process of moving from vision to study to strategies to implementation. Simply put, the destination is a transformed church.

It is St. Barnabas' Church, a corporate-sized parish where the rector and vestry engaged in a year-long process of scripture study and self-discovery, renewed its commitment to its music ministry, and initiated a capital campaign to expand its facilities to reflect this focus. At the same time, the parish explored ways to become more intentional about its newcomer integration process. By the time a direct pledge increase was sought, the congregation had been well prepared, and they made it clear that they supported these priorities. The pledge drive was a success, with an increase in existing pledges and many new pledges from those who now felt welcome and a part of the whole. And they have not stopped there, but have begun looking at how best to use their expertise in music to bring more people into their fellowship, while also rating their outreach programs and keeping only those that make sense at this time.

◆ ◆ ◆ ◆ ◆

It is Grace Church, a pastoral-sized parish located at the far reaches of its diocese, like several smaller churches nearby that belong to other neighboring dioceses. The rector and vestry initiated a "Year of Grace," in which they determined three areas of focus for their energies: community outreach, youth and families, and newcomer recruitment. For each area, they considered what they were doing well already and how to improve these, and then moved on to a few new things that they could do. For example, under community outreach, they counted seven programs in which they were currently engaged, ranging from a food bank and clean water program to work with the local detention center. They decided that there could also be ways of interacting with their community by sponsoring a "nurse appreciation" event and becoming involved with their local high school and middle school. Likewise, they looked at their acolytes and became more intentional in training them in other areas of parish ministry, as well as rewarding their hard work with more social occasions and trips, including participation in the National Acolyte Festival in Washington, D.C. They also began exploring new programs to support families, such as a group "date night" for parents complete with supervised childcare and activities at the church, a marriage enrichment program, and a congratulatory section in each parish newsletter devoted to the accomplishments of their young people. In these and other ways, the people of Grace Church began to feel like they belonged to a new church, full of renewed energy and vision. Pledging increased and a planned giving program was initiated. They even became the foundation of an innovative cross-diocesan coalition with the other congregations nearby, obtaining grants to help in training events and shared marketing plans.

◆ ◆ ◆ ◆ ◆

It is St. Andrew's, a small church in an area where the Spanish-speaking population is outnumbering those for whom English is a first language. Here, self-study resulted in three primary areas of focus, including community involvement, worship, and new membership retention and recruitment. The all-Anglo leadership began to step outside their own comfort zone and consider what new forms of worship might be required if they were to be stewards of their community. They became serious about praying regularly for newcomers as well as for their community, and they designated funds for handicap accessibility.

◆ ◆ ◆ ◆ ◆

It is All Saints' Church, a large, program-sized parish in an over fifty-five planned community where the rector decided to challenge the people to consider new ways that they could make a difference and not simply "ride out" their years. A significant facilities expansion program commenced, with realistic goals that made the entire campus entirely accessible to persons with disabilities, but also with space for a nursery and children's Sunday school program. These were created with an eye toward both visiting grandchildren for parishioners and the increase of young families moving into the area immediately around the planned community. The parish leadership decided that theirs could be the church of surrogate grandparents for these new residents, reaching out intentionally to them while honoring their own history as a fifty-five–plus community. They even spent some funds to create a business card-sized CD-ROM with information and interviews about the parish, as a fun conversation piece for parishioners to give away to people they would meet. It was a technologically savvy and stereotype-challenging move for a "seniors" congregation to make, and highly popular.

♦ ♦ ♦ ♦ ♦

It is St. Paul's Church, a tiny, family-sized congregation in an area that shows no signs of a possibility of population increase. And yet, because of the historical significance of the town, thousands of tourists flock to it, and parish leaders began to take notice. Drawing on the example of some historic Anglican cathedrals in England, they decided to make "tourism ministry" an important part of their identity and vision of stewardship, offering not only their usual Sunday morning service in contemporary English for their small but committed residential congregation, but also a Saturday afternoon service for tourists. They decided to use the Prayer Book service of a century past and to dress in period-costume for this service, which is still very much a time of living worship but also ties in directly with the very reason the tourists are present. Each visitor is given a booklet on the historical significance of the church and invited to write the name of a departed loved one in a special book of remembrance; the names are remembered in prayer on that same day throughout the years to come. Lay members trained in pastoral care are also assigned to be available to any visitor who wishes to pray quietly for strength or hope in his or her own life. All these visitors contribute because they are now a part of this historical, living church.

♦ ♦ ♦ ♦ ♦

It is the Church of the Transfiguration, a church in a resort community where at one time the clergy position had been a part-time position. But the new priest began to inspire the lay leaders to think of their threefold ministry with their residents, their visitors, and other area faith-based communities. In an area where people can come and go, the rector made clear, solid, scriptural teaching a foundational piece of congregational life. A new focus on families and youth has enlivened the congregation, and direct asking for projects of growth and improvements have met with success.

♦   ♦   ♦   ♦   ♦

It is St. Stephen's Church, a pastoral-sized congregation in a community that has experienced massive change in recent years, moving from a historic center to a university town. Long considered on the periphery of the diocese, clergy and lay leaders began to find ways to attend and even host diocesan events, raise their giving to the diocese, and become more in tune with what was happening outside their walls. Similarly, they began to explore what it would mean to become a "church for the community" and promoted community services while becoming more involved in other community networks. New part-time staff positions for children and youth were added, as well as fresh programming for various events during the week—a Celtic worship service, a natural spirituality course, even experimental programs for young people— and as a result the parish began to attract new people and new contributions.

♦   ♦   ♦   ♦   ♦

It is St. John's, a church that had experienced great hurt because of divisive issues, but where parish leaders were now focusing on the nurturing of new leaders, hosting small-group breakfast studies during the week, teaching foundational courses on what it means to follow Christ in the Episcopal tradition, and advertising themselves as "a church where your name is known and your gifts are utilized." An old storage room was converted into a children's chapel, and a formerly rented house out back became the "youth house," where young people could gather in their own space. Wounds of the past were recognized openly, but the focus was given to health and vitality for the future. "Join us as we move forward in love and life," became the watchword, and newly coached leaders began to move into positions where they could make a difference.

◆　◆　◆　◆　◆

And since it is not only churches that need to be transformed, but dioceses and other regional structures as well, as they offer much-needed support to the parochial front lines of ministry, it is also the Diocese of Arizona, where the bishop's goal of ten new churches in ten years required new initiatives like the Alleluia Fund, partnerships with national groups to help parishes with capital campaigns and planned giving, "new growth initiative" grants to assist existing congregations with specific projects, and new ways of doing business through convention seminars and regional "staff road shows."

It is the Diocese of Kansas, where a staff person with experience in funding initiatives was hired to help with development needs, training church members in annual pledging and planned giving and bringing in capital fundraising support.

It is the Diocese of Vermont, where a staff person with an impressive track record in stewardship has been hired and placed in a location other than the diocesan headquarters as a reminder that the diocese is more than the "see city," and to promote expanded regional connections and leadership.

It is the denominational seminary where stewardship is being included in the curriculum as a vital aspect of ministerial formation. It is the regional province where training opportunities are being offered in order to equip dioceses with stewardship tools. Above all, it is my church. It is your church. It is any church that has decided to lay its foundation on the solid ground of gospel hope and redemptive love. It is every church that takes seriously the call to produce disciples and leaders, not simply attendees. It is a Church of the Wise where leaders combine profound study with practical strategy.

At various times, I have used in Communion services the following anonymous words of invitation to the Table: "Come to the Table of Christ, not because you are perfect, but because you are loved; not because you have arrived, but because God is with you on the journey." For all of us who desire to grow as holistic stewards, who desire to be a Barnabas in our own twenty-first-century context, this is our divine invitation to be transformed.

# A Guide for Discussion

You may of course read the books in this series on your own, but because they focus on the transformation of the Episcopal Church in the twenty-first century, the books are especially useful as a basis for discussion and reflection within a congregation or community. The questions below are intended to generate fruitful discussion about an experience of the Bible in the congregations with which members of the group are familiar.

Each group will identify its own needs and will be shaped by the interests of the participants and their comfort in sharing personal life stories. Discussion leaders will wish to focus on particular areas that address the concerns and goals of the group, using the questions and themes provided here simply as suggestions for a place to start the conversation.

# The Current Landscape

In this chapter Robertson compares stewardship patterns in the Church of the Wise and the Church of the Foolish.

 ✦ In what ways does your congregation resemble the Church of the Wise in its approach to stewardship?

 ✦ In what ways does your congregation resemble the Church of the Foolish in its approach to stewardship?

✦　✦　✦　✦　✦

Researchers have identified a number of different understandings of stewardship among the several generational groups that are found in most parishes. Robertson believes that "a pledge program or capital campaign that works for someone in their sixties will not likely work for someone in their forties, much less someone in their twenties" (page 5).

 ✦ What generational groups do you see in your congregation? Which ones are the largest? Which ones exercise the most power in decision-making?

 ✦ Does your congregation use a "one-size-fits-all" approach to stewardship, or does it adapt its stewardship plan according to the various age groups of the members? How could you tell?

 ✦ If your congregation uses the "one-size-fits-all" approach, to which generational group(s) are stewardship materials generally addressed—in tone, mode of approach, and choice of themes?

## Tour Guides

In this chapter Robertson explores some of the scriptural foundations for a Christian understanding of stewardship.

* Read chapter 12 of Luke's gospel, considering each of the sections identified by Robertson on page 31. How would you describe Jesus' views of material possessions—his "theology of stewardship"?

* Which aspects of Jesus' understanding of material possessions do you find appealing? difficult or confusing? offensive? impossible to live out?

* Where do you see individuals or communities, either in history or today, living out a relationship with material possessions that resembles the principles Jesus describes?

♦    ♦    ♦    ♦    ♦

Robertson concludes the chapter with the question, "What, then, does it mean to be a faithful and wise steward?" (page 48).

* How would you answer his question?

* What "tour guides" or mentors, past and present, have informed the development of your relationship with material possessions—your "theology of stewardship"?

# Suggested Route and Tools for the Journey

In these two chapters Robertson explores his "Barnabas plan" for stewardship and offers tools for implementing it. Imagine how such a plan might look in your congregation by considering the following questions.

+ *Begin with the big picture:* How might you gather answers to the fundamental question of why your church exists? What are the important moments in its history? What are important elements of its mission today?

+ *Arrange structures strategically:* In what ways do your current structures reflect your priorities in mission? What is missing? How might a mutual ministry review be practiced in your congregation? What questions need to be asked?

+ *Retain and recruit newcomers:* How are newcomers welcomed and integrated into your congregation? What might prevent visitors from finding your church? What might encourage them to come back? What might discourage them from becoming members?

+ *Nurture fellow leaders and stewards:* How is leadership shared in your congregation? In what ways are future leaders nurtured and trained? How do you identify what gifts are not being fully utilized?

+ *Ask for direction and support:* How is prayer incorporated into the stewardship plan of your congregation? How is the wisdom of former leaders and long-time members valued and heard?

- *Budget with vision:* How are budgets developed in your congregation? Who has input, and when? Does your budget reflect your shared vision and mission?

- *Analyze giving patterns:* How is pledging evaluated in your congregation? Who analyzes the data, and how is it shared with the members? Consider how the analysis forms in Tool 7 might be useful in your congregation.

- *Specify a strategic pledging plan:* How are stewardship plans developed in your congregation? In what ways are they effective? Where do they fall short?

◆  ◆  ◆  ◆  ◆

Robertson describes in some detail his vision of an ACTS Commission that is responsible for many of the tasks involved in a stewardship plan.

- What might an ACTS Commission look like in your congregation? What would some of the obstacles be to forming such a commission? How would it resemble current or past stewardship committees?

- How might you make stewardship a year-round program in your congregation?

- How could you personalize your pledge program to address different groups within the congregation? Are children and youth currently included in your stewardship plan? How are new members taught about financial matters?

- Is planned giving part of your stewardship plan?

## The Destination

In this chapter Robertson describes a number of churches that have been transformed and renewed through their work in developing a more holistic understanding of stewardship as part of their identity as Christ's ambassadors in the world, rather than seeing stewardship as a once-a-year plea to increase pledging.

* Which congregations and dioceses described here resemble most closely your own?

* If you were to add a description of the stewardship journey of your congregation during the past twenty years to Robertson's list, what would you write?

* Now imagine what your congregation might look like in five years if a revitalizing holistic stewardship program were implemented. How would you write that story of your congregation for Robertson's list?

♦  ♦  ♦  ♦  ♦

Robertson concludes this chapter with an invitation to Holy Communion that reminds us all that "God is with [us] on the journey" (page 154).

* How does it change your sense of the work of a parish stewardship or finance committee when you hear this reminder? What difference does it make to you that God accompanies those who undertake that responsibility?

* What are some of the concrete ways that God accompanies us on the journey?

# Resources

## books and printed materials

Amerson, Melvin. *Stewardship in African-American Churches: A New Paradigm.* Nashville: Discipleship Resources, 2006.

Barna, George. *Revolution.* Carol Stream, Ill.: Tyndale, 2005.

———. *How to Increase Giving in Your Church.* Ventura, Calif.: Gospel Light Publications, 1997.

———. *User Friendly Churches: What Christians Need to Know About the Churches People Love to Go to.* Ventura, Calif.: Gospel Light Publications, 1991.

———. *The Frog in the Kettle.* Ventura, Calif.: Gospel Light Publications, 1990.

Bellesi, Denny and Leesa. *The Kingdom Assignment.* Grand Rapids: Zondervan, 2001.

Brown, Keith. *On the Road Again: Managing Evangelism and Stewardship.* New York: Church Publishing, 2001.

Callahan, Kennon L. *Giving and Stewardship in an Effective Church.* San Francisco: Jossey-Bass, 1997.

Christopher, J. Clif. *Not Your Parents' Offering Plate: A New Vision for Financial Stewardship.* Nashville: Abingdon, 2008.

Cloughen, Charles. *One-Minute Stewardship Sermons.* Harrisburg: Morehouse, 1997.

Croft, Steven. *Ministry in Three Dimensions.* London: Darton Longman & Todd, 1999.

Dick, Dan R. *Revolutionizing Christian Stewardship for the 21st Century: Lessons from Copernicus.* Nashville: Discipleship Resources, 1998.

Durall, Michael. *Creating Congregations of Generous People.* Herndon, Va.: Alban Institute, 1999.

Episcopal Media Center. *Living with Money.* Harrisburg: Morehouse, 2003.

Gearing, Charles E., Frederick Osborn III, and Pamela S. Wesley. *Funding Future Ministry.* New York: Episcopal Church Foundation, 2000.

Gossen, Thomas R. *Joyful Giving: A Manual for Stewardship Development.* Third edition. Wichita, Ks.: TENS Publishing, 2007.

Hueckel, Sharon. *Stewardship by the Book: Bulletin Bits Based on the Sunday Readings.* Huntington, Ind.: Our Sunday Visitor Publishing, 2004.

Hurley-Pitts, Michael. *The Passionate Steward: Recovering Christian Stewardship from Secular Fundraising.* New York: St. Brigid Press, 2006.

Martin, Alfred. *Biblical Stewardship.* Dubuque: ECS, 2005.

Martin, Kevin. *Stewardship and Giving.* Wichita, Ks.: TENS Publishing, 2001.

McNaughton, John. *More Blessed to Give.* New York: Church Publishing, 2003.

Mead, Loren B. *Transforming Congregations for the Future.* Herndon, Va.: Alban Institute, 1994.

Miller, Herb. *New Consecration Sunday Stewardship Program: Team Member Manual.* Nashville: Abingdon, 2002.

Powell, Mark Allan. *Giving to God: The Bible's Good News about Living a Generous Life.* Grand Rapids: Eerdmans, 2006.

Robertson, C. K., ed. *Religion and Sexuality: Passionate Debates.* New York: Peter Lang, 2006.

————. *Religion as Entertainment.* New York: Peter Lang, 2002.

Schaller, Lyle E. *The Seven-Day-a-Week Church.* Nashville: Abingdon, 1992.

Schwarz, Christian A. *Natural Church Development.* Sixth edition. St. Charles, Ill.: Church Smart Resources, 2003.

Strobel, Lee. *Inside the Mind of Unchurched Harry and Mary.* Grand Rapids: Zondervan, 1993.

Tyler, Michael D. and Jennifer. *Faith and Money: Understanding Annual Giving in the Church.* Nashville: Discipleship Resources, 2003.

Vincent, Mark. *A Christian View of Money: Celebrating God's Generosity.* Scottdale, Penn.: Herald Press, 1997.

Warren, Rick, Chip Ingram, Ron Blue, Howard Dayton, and Chuck Bentley. *Managing our Finances God's Way: Small Group Study Guide and Workbook.* Forest, Calif.: Purpose-Driven Publishing, 2006.

Westerhoff, John H. *Grateful and Generous Hearts.* Harrisburg: Morehouse, 1997.

Wilson, Charles R. and Lynne Davenport. *Against All Odds: Ten Stories of Vitality in Small Churches.* Laramie, Wy.: Jethro, 1982.

Wright, Lauren. *Giving—The Sacred Art: Creating a Lifestyle of Generosity.* Woodstock, Vt.: SkyLight Paths, 2008.

Zech, Charles E. *Best Practices in Parish Stewardship.* Huntington, Ind.: Our Sunday Visitor Publishing, 2008.

www.endowedparishes.org
The Consortium of Endowed Episcopal Parishes (CEEP) website offers information on conferences, resources, and best practices around endowments, mission, and stewardship.

www.episcopalchurch.org/stewardship
The official website of the Episcopal Church offers among its many resources a section on stewardship, with congregational assessment tools, financial commitment programs, year-round stewardship information, and stewardship education for children.

www.tens.org
The Episcopal Network for Stewardship (TENS) website has excellent resources on stewardship for parishes, including books, conferences, and best practices.

# Notes

1. George Barna, *The Frog in the Kettle* (Ventura, Calif.: Gospel Light Publications, 1990), 133.
2. Loren B. Mead, *Transforming Congregations for the Future* (Herndon, Va.: Alban Institute, 1994), 16, 23, 100.
3. Lee Strobel, *Inside the Mind of Unchurched Harry and Mary* (Grand Rapids, Mich.: Zondervan, 1993), 44–45.
4. Steven Croft, *Ministry in Three Dimensions* (London: Darton Longman & Todd, 1999), 9, 20, 28.
5. Charles R. Wilson and Lynne Davenport, *Against All Odds: Ten Stories of Vitality in Small Churches* (Frenchtown, N.J.: Jethro Publications, 1982), 128.
6. *Acts: From Maintenance to Mission* by C. K. Robertson and Susan Snook is available at www.tens.org.